DOGS

500 QUESTIONS ANSWERED

DOGS

500 QUESTIONS ANSWERED

Caroline Davis

First published in Great Britain in 2005 by
Hamlyn, a division of Octopus Publishing Group Ltd

This edition published in 2007 by Bounty Books,
a division of Octopus Publishing Group Ltd,
2–4 Heron Quays, London E14 4JP

ISBN-13: 978-0-753715-18-5
ISBN-10: 0-7537-1518-X

A CIP catalogue record for this book is available
from the British Library.

Printed and bound in China

Notes
The advice given here should not be used as a
substitute for that of a veterinary surgeon. No dogs
or puppies were harmed in the making of this book.

In this book, unless the information given is
specifically for female dogs, dogs are referred to
throughout as 'he'. The information is equally
applicable to both male and female dogs, unless
otherwise specified.

Contents

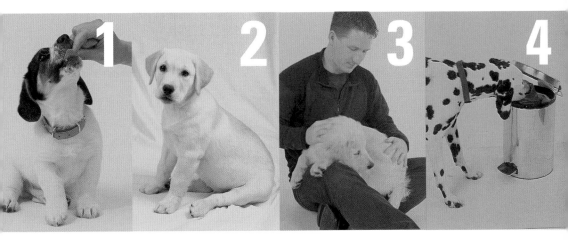

Introduction

Dogs are incredibly versatile creatures. Not only can they make wonderful companions, they also play a huge part in many people's lives as a means of employment, to maintain law and order, to provide invaluable help to rescue services, and to enable some disadvantaged humans to regain self-respect, to enjoy life, and find work. For some people, their sole comfort is their dog. In addition, many breeds still fulfil their original roles as livestock herders and watchdogs.

However, to get the most out of a relationship with a dog, it helps to know why dogs do the things they do. Understanding the canine language, and enabling your pet to understand you and what you want from him, will promote a more rewarding and fulfilling partnership.

Have you ever wanted to know, for example, why dogs turn round and round before settling down to sleep, 'misbehave', and chase the vacuum cleaner, or if they suffer the effects of passive smoking? Then look no further. In this book, I hope to provide – with a common-sense and practical approach – the know-how required to increase your understanding of canine behaviour, solve common problems, and discover all those things you want to know about dogs but are, perhaps, afraid to ask for fear of being thought 'stupid'.

If I have succeeded, your dog will be grateful that you took the time to read this book and cared enough for him to follow the advice offered. If I have omitted the exact question you are asking yourself, then I apologize – but I hope you will use what I have provided as a stepping-stone to seek further information about a particular subject, for both your and your pet's benefit. I, too, am always learning new things about dogs I didn't know before.

This book is for all the dogs I have been privileged to meet, own and care for. It is also for those dog owners who wish to seek an answer to their query, never stop wanting to learn more about dogs, and are willing to follow sound advice in an effort to improve and enhance the relationship with their canine best friend. Most of all, it is for the benefit of all dogs everywhere.

Caroline Davis

1

Choosing a dog

Exactly how many breeds of dog are there?

According to the UK's Kennel Club, there are over 450 known breeds of dog worldwide. Some of these are unknown outside their country of origin, and not all breeds are recognized by the official organizations that oversee breeding and showing. Being unrecognized by an organization means that those breeds cannot be shown under its rules.

At the time of writing, the three main canine organizations are the British Kennel Club (KC) which recognizes 202 breeds of dog, the American Kennel Club (AKC) which recognizes 150, and the Fédération Cynologique International (FCI), based in Belgium, which recognizes 311.

Why are there so many breeds?

Archaeological finds around the world suggest that selective breeding was first carried out by man some 10,000 years ago. The aim was to produce different types of dog for varied tasks and different purposes, including hunting, herding, guarding, hauling loads, fighting and, of course, acting as companions.

Later came breeding between different types and sizes of dog for aesthetic reasons as well as for very specific requirements, such as small terriers like the Jack Russell for hunting quarry underground, small lapdogs like the Pekinese to be used as 'hand-warmers', and massive, fierce-looking dogs like the

Mastiff as guards. More breeds evolved from crossing cross-breeds, so that today we have a huge variety, although the basic model remains the same.

How did the different breeds evolve?

The origins of dogs can be traced back some 40 million years, to a weasel-like carnivorous mammal called *Miacis*. About

12,000 years ago, wolves (and also foxes, jackals and coyotes) evolved, in the form in which they appear today.

According to R. I. Pocock, who determined the information in 1935, modern-day dogs (*Canis familiaris*) are derived from four types of wolf (*Canis lupus*): the northern grey wolf, the pale-footed Asian wolf, the small desert wolf of Arabia, and the woolly-coated wolf of Tibet and northern India. Pocock suggested that these four types of wolf

CLOCKWISE FROM TOP LEFT St Bernard, Kooikerhondje, Afghan Hound, Anatolian Shepherd Dog, Akita, Griffon Bruxellois. The selection of breeds available is large and varied, with each breed displaying different characteristics.

contained the genes necessary to develop all modern breeds of dog.

Modern breeds were developed by man, taking a limited number of dogs and breeding them so as to fix a distinct appearance and/or behaviour.

ABOVE **A native of Mexico, the tiny Chihuahua was named after the state in which it originated.**

ABOVE **Many myths surround the Irish Wolfhound. One of the most famous originated in the 13th century in north Wales, where a village is said to be named after Prince Llewelyn's favourite hound, Gelert. The dog's grave was marked by a mound of stones and became known in Welsh as Beddgelert, meaning Gelert's grave.**

I like tiny, cute dogs. Which are the smallest breeds?

The Chihuahua is the world's smallest breed. Second is the Miniature Dachshund. There have been smaller dogs of other breeds, but these are anomalies. The smallest dog in the *Guinness Book of World Records* is Whitney, a Yorkshire Terrier in the UK who is 7.6 cm (3 in) to the shoulder.

Which is the tallest breed?

The Irish Wolfhound is the world's tallest dog. Close to it are the Deerhound (formerly known as the Scottish Deerhound) and the Great Dane. Minimum/ideal heights are shown in the table opposite.

SMALLEST BREEDS

Chihuahua	16–20 cm (6½–8 in)
Miniature Dachshund	12–23 cm (5–9 in)
Pekinese	15–23 cm (6–9 in)
Griffon Bruxellois	17.5–20 cm (7–8 in)
Dandie Dinmont	20–27 cm (8–11 in)

I would like a big, chunky dog – which breeds fulfil my criteria?

The heaviest breed is the St Bernard.
Japanese Fighting Dogs (Tosa Inu, also known as the 'sumo wrestler' of the dog world) bred in the West run a close second, although traditionally bred Tosas in their native country are considerably lighter.

Which are the lightest breeds?

The Chihuahua is not only the smallest breed in the world, it is also the lightest.
All the smallest breeds shown in the table are classified as 'Toy' and are extremely popular as affectionate lapdogs. However, they also make good watchdogs, are intelligent, lively and very courageous (sometimes to the point of foolhardiness), and have been characterized as 'little dogs with the hearts and minds of lions'. They make great pets, but are equally at home 'helping' around the farm.

ABOVE Due to the introduction of Newfoundland blood to increase the size of the breed in the 19th century, St Bernards can be either long- or short-coated.

TALLEST BREEDS

	USA	UK
Irish Wolfhound	81 cm (32 in)	79 cm (31 in)
Great Dane	76–81 cm (30–32 in)	76 cm (30 in)
Deerhound	76 cm (30 in)	76 cm (30 in)
Greyhound	76 cm (30 in)	71–76 cm (28–30 in)
Anatolian Shepherd	74 cm (29 in)	74–81 cm (29–32 in)
Leonberger	72–80 cm (28¼–31½ in)	72–80 cm (28¼–31½ in)
Borzoi	71 cm (28 in)	74 cm (29 in)
Pyrenean Mountain Dog	67.7–81 cm (27–32 in)	70 cm (27½ in)

HEAVIEST BREEDS

St Bernard	48.6–90 kg (110–200 lb)
Japanese Fighting Dog	45–90 kg (100–200 lb) (West)
	30–40 kg (66–88 lb) (Japan)
Mastiff	86 kg (190 lb)
Tibetan Mastiff	81.6 kg (180 lb)
Pyrenean Mastiff	70 kg (155 lb)

LIGHTEST BREEDS

Chihuahua	0.5–2.7 kg (1–6 lb)
Pomeranian	1.3–3.3 kg (3–7½ lb)
Yorkshire Terrier	3.1 kg (6¾ lb)
Japanese Chin	3.1 kg (6¾ lb)
Maltese	1.8–3.2 kg (4–7 lb)
Papillon	4.9 kg (11 lb)

Which breeds do not live long?

Due to advances in veterinary medicine, dogs are living longer than they used to. However, large, heavy dogs have a shorter lifespan than their small, light counterparts due to their genetic make-up, as well as their bodies being subjected to more wear and tear. Non-pedigrees tend to live longer than purebreds.

Some breeds are known to have a limited lifespan due to their sheer size (such as the Irish Wolfhound and St Bernard), hereditary defects, susceptibility to certain ailments and/or conformation.

Which are the longest-lived breeds?

Studies into canine longevity provide varying results. A Danish veterinary study discovered that Shetland Sheepdogs, Dachshunds and Poodles fared well in the age stakes, usually exceeding 12 years, while a UK study revealed that Jack Russell Terriers, Whippets and Miniature Poodles are particularly long-lived at over 13 years. The UK research seems to suggest that smaller dogs may have a slight edge in the longevity stakes.

How old are dogs compared to humans?

At 6 months of age, a dog is the equivalent to a 7-year-old human. Both have a playful and inquisitive nature that tests behavioural boundaries. Comparing ages between dogs and humans is extremely difficult as it depends on the breed of dog; some have a shorter lifespan than others. But as an approximate guide only we can equate 14 human years to 1 year of a dog's life, and thereafter add 7 human years for each dog year. The graph opposite shows the correlation.

DOG AGES IN HUMAN TERMS

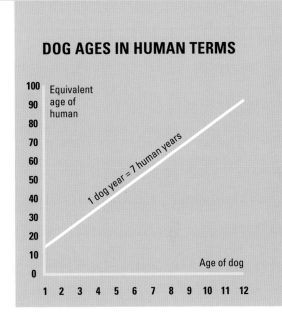

Equivalent age of human

1 dog year = 7 human years

Age of dog

LIMITED LONGEVITY (YEARS)

LONG-LIVED BREEDS (YEARS)

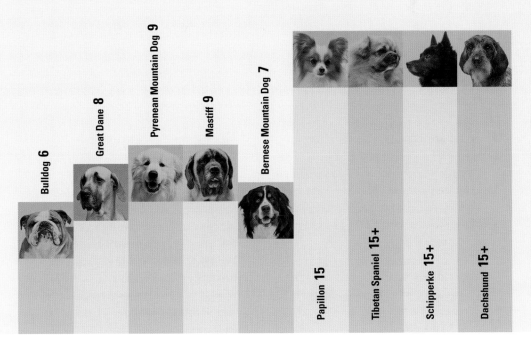

Bulldog **6**

Great Dane **8**

Pyrenean Mountain Dog **9**

Mastiff **9**

Bernese Mountain Dog **7**

Papillon **15**

Tibetan Spaniel **15+**

Schipperke **15+**

Dachshund **15+**

Which breeds should I consider as a small, gentle dog for my elderly parents?

There are plenty of small breeds, as well as non-pedigrees, with a kind and gentle nature. Your choice then depends on factors such as preferred coat type, environmental space and exercise requirements.

Pugs, Dachshunds, Chihuahuas, Pekinese and Pomeranians are all excellent lapdogs, although the latter two require daily grooming. English Toy Spaniels (Cavalier and King Charles Spaniels) make good pets, as do Poodles, Bichon Frises and Shih Tzus, but as well as daily grooming these breeds require specialized coat care.

All these dogs are happy with as much or as little exercise as their owner is able to give them. If plenty of daily exercise can be provided, the choice widens and it becomes more a case of which type of dog appeals, but avoid powerful or extremely energetic types.

I would really like a Greyhound or a Whippet. Do they need a lot of exercise?

Perhaps surprisingly, both Whippets and Greyhounds are happy to be couch potatoes if they have the chance. There are many Greyhounds retired from racing that are in need of a good home, and in return they make wonderfully affectionate companions that need little in the way of grooming or exercise. Greyhound rescue centres are usually only too happy to advise on the breed's care and requirements.

Both Greyhounds and Whippets will require at least one good gallop per day in addition to their leash walk, to satisfy their natural desire to run; this should be on level, smooth ground, due to their slender legs and feet and thin skin, all of which are prone to injury.

LEFT Like other sighthounds (see page 26), Whippets need to be socialized with other small household pets from puppyhood in order to quell their instinct to chase them.

ABOVE With a compatible cross-breed, such as this German Shepherd x Rottweiler, you can have the best of both types.

ABOVE RIGHT Pedigree dogs, like this Weimaraner, are bred to match a standard.

RIGHT Mongrels (non-pedigrees) come in all shapes, sizes and colours.

What's the difference between a pedigree, a cross-breed and a non-pedigree (mongrel)?

Pedigree dogs are those that are purebred (bred true to a set standard). Cross-breeds have pedigree parents of different breeds, while mongrels are dogs with one or both parents being cross-breeds or mongrels. Pedigree breeds have been formed by crossing one or more other breeds to produce a 'new design'.

Whether pedigree, cross-breed or mongrel, comparable sized dogs cost the same to feed and maintain.

ABOVE **Cavalier King Charles Spaniels are delightful little dogs and are renowned for being good with children. They make ideal family pets.**

Which breed is most suitable as a child-orientated family pet?

The majority of breeds make good family pets, with a few exceptions (see page 42). Your choice will then depend on size, exercise and coat-care requirements. For low exercise and coat maintenance the Basset Hound and Greyhound are ideal, while for those willing to provide sufficient exercise the Labrador Retriever, German Shepherd Dog, and Border Collie are popular choices.

If you can cope with regular grooming and professional coat maintenance, the Rough Collie, English Toy Spaniels (Cavalier and King Charles Spaniels), Golden Retriever, Finnish Spitz, German Spitz, Shih Tzu, Lhasa Apso and Bichon Frise all fulfil the criteria.

AVAILABILITY AND COST

SOURCE	COST
Pedigree breeder	Prices vary enormously depending on the breed, so it pays to shop around to ensure you choose a healthy puppy/adult that has been properly socialized. Show-quality animals cost more.
Friends and family	Non-pedigrees are often free, while pedigrees and cross-breeds vary in cost.
Rescue centre	Expect to pay a modest charge to cover neutering and vaccination fees.
Strays	Free, although there may be veterinary costs for de-fleaing, vaccinations and so on.
Pet store/puppy farm (puppy mill)	Prices vary depending on the outlet and area. Pedigrees cost more than non-pedigrees and cross-breeds.

Where can I get a dog and how much will it cost?

There are several sources for pet dogs. These are shown in the table opposite. Whatever source you choose, ensure that the conditions in which the dogs are kept are clean and that the animals appear healthy, socialized with people (as far as their ages allow) and happy. It is also essential to be certain that puppies are fully weaned and ready to leave their mother, which is usually at not less than 8 weeks old.

Which are the most expensive dogs?

Expense falls into two categories: the initial outlay on the dog and any necessary equipment, and maintenance costs throughout its lifetime. The less common breeds tend to be more expensive to purchase. Rather than buy a dog on looks or price alone, take into account whether that breed is more prone to accident or ailment than others. Pet insurers tend to base their premiums on the breed of dog and its age.

LEFT **The Dogue de Bordeaux and English Bulldog are among the more expensive breeds to buy.**

Is it better to get a male dog or a female?

This is really a matter of personal preference. If the dog is neutered, then the question of sex is less important as there will be little difference between males and females. How loving and obedient your pet will be depends on how it is brought up and treated by you, the owner.

If you wish your pet to remain entire (unneutered), then there are differences to consider. It is not true to say, as many believe, that a male (dog) is less 'trouble' than a female (bitch), or that bitches are more predictable in temperament and make better pets, especially around children. See pages 72–73 for more information on neutering.

Why do dogs' shapes vary so much?

Dog shapes and sizes usually reflect the primary purpose for which they were bred.
● **Slim, athletic and deep-chested** For sprinting after quarry.
● **Rangy and deep-chested** For stamina while hunting, or for herding.
● **Close-coupled and heavy-muscled** For pulling loads, guarding and/or fighting.
● **Short-legged** For hunting quarry underground and so that hunters on foot can keep up with them.
● **Tiny** For lapdogs. Some examples are shown in the table on page 20.

In addition, many breeds have been developed simply for their appearance, particularly the more luxuriantly coated or unusual Toy types.

BREED PURPOSES

Breed	Load-pulling strength	Distance, speed and endurance	Short-distance speed	Herding	Guarding ability	Stamina	Suitability as a companion
Saluki			●				●
Siberian Husky	●	●				●	●
English Foxhound		●				●	
Pekinese							●
Newfoundland	●				●	●	●
German Shepherd Dog		●		●	●	●	●

Do non-pedigree dogs enjoy better health and live longer than pedigrees?

Research has shown that mixed breeds tend to live longer than many pedigree breeds. However, as with purebreds, large, heavily built non-pedigrees tend to have a shorter lifespan than their smaller, lighter counterparts (see pages 14–15).

Generally, non-pedigrees suffer fewer problems than pedigree dogs as the gene pool is not so limited. Many pedigree breeds are prone to hereditary health problems or ailments (see page 40), which have a bearing on their lifespan.

Interestingly, through comparing claims one pet insurance company has found that English Setters, Jack Russell Terriers, English Springer Spaniels and cross-bred Poodles tend to be healthier than other pedigrees.

Which are the fastest breeds of dog?

Over short distances, the Greyhound reigns supreme. One of the breed has been clocked at 72 kmph (45 mph) on a racetrack, making it the second-fastest animal in the world next to the cheetah. Other speedy sighthounds include the Whippet, Saluki and Afghan Hound, and any other canines with a similar light, athletic build.

The Border Collie is the fastest dog in the agility field, at which this breed excels, while the Siberian Husky is the fastest load-pulling endurance breed over great distances.

I am elderly and would prefer a sedate, slow-moving dog. Which breeds will suit me?

Heavy dogs with short stumpy legs, such as the Basset Hound and Bulldog, are the slowest. Other heavily built breeds that tend to be sedate in movement include the Clumber Spaniel, Sussex Spaniel, St Bernard and Old English Mastiff. Certain Toy breeds, such as the Pekinese, are slow movers because their legs are short.

Consider your surroundings when choosing a suitable breed. Long-backed, short-legged breeds, such as the Basset Hound, are prone to back injuries, so negotiating stairs is not good for them. Polished wooden flooring is also not good for dogs, as they can easily slip on it and injure themselves.

BELOW LEFT The sleek, elegant Greyhound has always been highly valued as both a courser (pursuer of small game) and a racing dog, with prime specimens commanding exceptionally high prices.

BELOW A big dog on little legs, the Basset Hound is the ideal companion for an owner who likes walks at a leisurely pace.

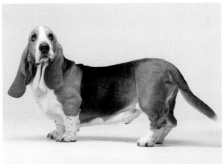

Why are some breeds harder to find than others?

Less popular breeds, such as the Sealyham, are harder to find because there simply is not the demand for them. They are therefore rarely seen outside the show ring. Conversely, a puppy from the more popular breeds can be difficult to source simply because of high demand, so you may have to order a puppy from a breeder and then wait until one becomes available, or be prepared to travel further afield to purchase one.

Because they are relatively unknown, breeds such as the Portuguese Water Dog are rarely seen outside their country of origin, and those rarer breeds that are to be found tend to be expensive because of their limited number.

Which is the most popular breed?

Number one in the canine top 10 in the UK, Canada and the USA, by registration figures, is the Labrador Retriever. The top 10 breeds in various countries are shown in the table opposite.

How can I find a reputable dog breeder?

Word of mouth is always a good way to find a source for the canine companion of your dreams. If you see a dog you like the look of, if possible ask the owner where they got him from and if they have had any temperament, behaviour or health problems with their pet. If the feedback is positive, then investigate further by contacting the breeders and arranging to visit their premises and view their dogs. This will give you the chance to meet the breeder, to form an opinion of them and their setup, and see for yourself whether they look after their animals properly and produce happy, healthy stock.

Veterinary surgeries are another good source of information, as they may well have experience of breeders in their area and know which ones are reputable and and reliable.

LEFT **The sensible but fun-loving Labrador Retriever is renowned as a devoted family pet.**

Are there any breeds that don't shed their coats or smell 'doggy'?

Dogs with oily coats, such as the Curly Coated Retriever, may have a distinctive 'doggy' smell, especially when wet.

However, any breed will carry an odour if the coat and skin are not kept clean.

Breeds with minimal coat odour and shedding include the Basenji, Kerry Blue Terrier, Poodle, Saluki, Whippet and Chinese Crested. The Italian Greyhound is another clean little dog; it rarely

TOP 10 BREEDS FROM AROUND THE WORLD

Rankings based on the number of registrations

The Kennel Club of Great Britain
1 Labrador Retriever; 2 German Shepherd Dog; 3 Cocker Spaniel; 4 English Springer Spaniel; 5 Staffordshire Bull Terrier; 6 Golden Retriever; 7 Cavalier King Charles Spaniel; 8 West Highland White Terrier; 9 Boxer; 10 Border Terrier.

American Kennel Club
1 Labrador Retriever; 2 Golden Retriever; 3 Beagle; 4 German Shepherd Dog; 5 Dachshund; 6 Yorkshire Terrier; 7 Boxer; 8 Poodle; 9 Shih Tzu; 10 Chihuahua.

The Canadian Kennel Club
1 Labrador Retriever; 2 Golden Retriever; 3 German Shepherd Dog; 4 Poodle; 5 Shetland Sheepdog; 6 Miniature Schnauzer; 7 Yorkshire Terrier; 8 Beagle; 9 Bichon Frise; 10 Shih Tzu.

New Zealand Kennel Club
1 Labrador Retriever; 2 German Shepherd Dog; 3 Golden Retriever; 4 Border Collie; 5 Boxer; 6 Rottweiler; 7 Bulldog; 8 Staffordshire Bull Terrier; 9 Bull Mastiff; 10 Cavalier King Charles Spaniel.

Dansk Kennel Klub (Danish Kennel Club)
1 German Shepherd Dog; 2 Labrador Retriever; 3 Golden Retriever; 4 German Wirehaired Pointer; 5 Wirehaired Dachshund; 6 Rottweiler; 7 Cairn Terrier; 8 West Highland White Terrier; 9 Flat-coated Retriever; 10 English Cocker Spaniel.

Kennel Union of Southern Africa
1 Yorkshire Terrier; 2 Labrador Retriever; 3 Bulldog; 4 Bull Terrier; 5 Rottweiler; 6 Golden Retriever; 7 Staffordshire Bull Terrier; 8 Siberian Husky; 9 Miniature Schnauzer; 10 Bull Mastiff.

Russia Kynological Federation (Russian Kennel Club)
1 Central Asian Shepherd Dog; 2 German Shepherd Dog; 3 Rottweiler; 4 American Staffordshire Terrier; 5 Labrador Retriever; 6 Bulldog; 7 Dobermann; 8 Boxer; 9 Bernese Mountain Dog; 10 Chinese Crested Dog.

Verband für das Deutsche Hundewesen (German Kennel Club))
1 German Shepherd Dog; 2 Dachshund; 3 German Wirehaired Pointer; 4 Labrador Retriever; 5 Poodle; 6 English Cocker Spaniel; 7 Great Dane; 8 Boxer; 9 Golden Retriever; 10 Rottweiler.

Norsk Kennelklub (Norwegian Kennel Club)
1 German Shepherd Dog; 2 Norwegian Elkhound; 3 English Setter; 4 Border Collie; 5 Golden Retriever; 6 Rottweiler; 7 Gordon Setter; 8 Cavalier King Charles Spaniel; 9 Labrador Retriever; 10 Tibetan Spaniel.

Royal New South Wales Canine Council (Australia)
1 German Shepherd Dog; 2 Labrador Retriever; 3 Cavalier King Charles Spaniel; 4 Staffordshire Bull Terrier; 5 Golden Retriever; 6 Border Collie; 7 Jack Russell Terrier; 8 Cocker Spaniel; 9 Boxer; 10 Toy Poodle.

LEFT The Basenji is a particularly clean breed of dog – it washes itself like a cat.

Why are pedigree dogs split into different categories in different countries?

The different breed categories or groupings are based on the breed's original purpose. While the sporting category for each major kennel club in the world remains basically the same, the non-sporting groups differ greatly: some clubs place certain breeds into the group the animals were originally bred for, while others put them in the category they are primarily used for these days. For instance, what used to be a fighting dog could be placed in the Utility group by one club, but in Working by another if its primary function today is as a guard dog.

moults and is odourless, but is relatively fragile in build and sensitive of nature, so is not suitable for a busy, child-orientated household or for those who require a more robust pet.

BREED GROUPINGS

UK GROUPING	US GROUPING	PURPOSE
Gundog	Sporting	Assisting in flushing and retrieving game.
Terrier	Sporting	Going underground to flush out and kill vermin and small game.
Hound	Sporting	Hunting game by scent or sight.
Utility	Non-sporting	Breeds whose original purpose is now defunct.
Pastoral	Herding	Looking after livestock.
Toy	Toy	Companions to humans.
Working	Working	Assisting in pulling loads; guarding.

Are the breed standards for official canine organizations the same?

There may be some variations – for example, the ideal height and weight – in the breed standards set by official organizations in different countries. However, these do not adversely affect those owners who simply require a pet. A dog that is a couple of centimetres over or under the set standard may not win prizes in the show ring, but that does not matter if his primary purpose is as a loyal and loving companion.

Why are some breeds not recognized by official canine organizations?

This is because those breeds fail to meet the standard set by an organization. In order to define a standard, an organization researches a breed's historical background, the number of dogs in the country, their health and temperament, along with consistency of type and conformation. All of this is carried out over a substantial period before an organization is satisfied that the breed meets its criteria. Some breeds are so rare that no reasonable research can be carried out, or there is insufficient interest in the breed to make it viable.

The situation may vary between organizations. For example, the breeds Leonberger and Swedish Vallund are recognized by the UK Kennel Club but are not yet accepted by the American Kennel Club.

Which breed will best suit my lifestyle?

When choosing a dog, it is important to consider your home life, work situation and other family members' needs. Ask yourself the following questions to determine which breed would most suit your situation:
- **What size house do you live in?** In most cases, this will determine the size of the dog.
- **Are there children in the household?** If so, you need to look at gentle, fun-loving and placid-tempered dogs.
- **Is there a garden or yard in which the dog can self-exercise and play?** If not, choose a breed that requires minimal daily exercise, or be prepared to take your pet out for 30- to 60-minute walks at least three times a day.
- **How much exercise and training time per day can you provide?** If you fail to provide the dog with the minimum he requires to remain healthy, obedient and sane, then expect problems.
- **Are you house-proud?** If so, avoid heavy-shedding, extremely active and/or slobbery breeds. Can you put up with the odd natural accident without becoming stressed? If not, don't get a dog.

Which type of active watchdog would enjoy life on our smallholding, with other pets and livestock?

A number of breeds spring to mind. These include the Border Collie, German Shepherd Dog, Labrador and Golden

Retrievers, English Springer Spaniel, Hungarian Vizsla, Old English Sheepdog, Rhodesian Ridgeback and Standard Poodle. Good-natured and well-trained examples of each of these breeds make ideal country companions as well as keeping a keen eye out for intruders.

However, there are also many other breeds that would fulfil your criteria, depending on the coat type you prefer. Examples include the Giant Schnauzer, Rottweiler, Leonberger, Bearded, Rough and Smooth Collies, Briard, Belgian Shepherd Dog and Anatolian Shepherd.

Are some dogs more time-consuming to own than others?

Intelligent 'working' breeds tend to be demanding of their owners' time and attention. This is because these dogs were originally developed to be highly interactive with their owners and physically capable of always being ready to work, so they need plenty of exercise. Long-coated dogs need more time spent on grooming, while hounds and terriers can prove difficult to train.

While all these factors should be taken into consideration when choosing a pet, it is important to bear in mind that how you care for, handle, train and interact

with your chosen breed has a huge influence in determining how well your dog behaves and relates to you, other people and animals.

What do the terms 'sighthound' and 'scenthound' mean?

Both terms refer to hunting breeds, and mean exactly what they suggest. Sighthounds (also known as gazehounds) rely on their keen eyesight to spot prey, and on their speed to chase it and bring it down or within range of the handlers' guns. Scenthounds use their highly developed sense of smell to track and seek out prey, and then either hold it at bay for their handlers to deal with or catch it themselves.

RIGHT **Scenthounds have broader snouts than sighthounds, for maximum olfaction (scenting ability). The gentle Bloodhound has been used to track lost people as well as game, because having found its quarry it will not kill it.**

ABOVE **Although primarily a sighthound, the Pharaoh Hound also tracks quarry by scent.**

What is the difference between scenthounds and sighthounds?

Sighthounds are lean dogs with long legs, muscled forequarters and powerful hindquarters. They are tall with large, round eyes positioned at the front and top end of the skull to maximize their field of vision. Narrow in build to reduce wind resistance, they have a deep chest housing the heart and lungs to utilize maximum oxygen intake for sprinting over short distances. They are also more aloof with strangers than scenthounds. Typical examples are the Afghan Hound, Greyhound, Borzoi and Irish Wolfhound.

Scenthounds also feature deep chests for maximum respiratory and pulmonary function, but their overall conformation is more compact than that of their keener-eyed counterparts and they are usually shorter-legged. They carry more weight, so that they can draw on their bodies' reserves of stored nutrients in order to maintain pace over prolonged periods. Typical examples are the Basset Hound, Dachshund, English Foxhound and Beagle.

Why do some breeds need more exercise than others?

Exercise falls into two categories, mental and physical. The amount of each that a dog needs usually boils down to the job the breed was originally developed to do. Dogs bred to herd or hunt generally feel the need to be on the go much of the time, while those whose lives were not as constantly active tend to need less mental and physical stimulation.

Conformation also figures in the equation. Athletic, lean dogs featuring a medium-sized (mesocephalic) skull are livelier than heavy, squat, short-legged dogs with short, broad (brachycephalic) skulls (see page 32).

Exceptions to the rules tend to be the 'sprinters'. Because these 'racehorses' are of lean build, their bodies carry hardly any nutritional reserves, so once they've exhausted these in a brief but speedy burst of activity they slow down. Until they have rested and eaten in order to build up enough energy, they aren't in a hurry to be on the go again.

Do breeds have particular traits?

Breeds in the various groups tend to share the same characteristics. Bear in mind that there are always exceptions to the general rules.

LEFT The Dobermann is a breed that suffers both ear-cropping and tail-docking.

Why do some breeds have their ears cropped and/or tails docked?

There is no good reason for these mutilations – they are done simply to achieve a certain look. Cropped-eared breeds in the countries that allow it include the Great Dane, Miniature Pinscher, Griffon Bruxellois (Brussels Griffon), Schnauzer, Boxer and Boston Terrier, while docked breeds include the Rottweiler, Old English Sheepdog and Poodle.

These days, however, thankfully people are shying away from such mutilations (which should only be carried out by a veterinary surgeon, although many now refuse to carry out 'crops and docks'), so an increasing number of traditionally cropped/docked breeds are remaining as nature intended. Various countries have different views and laws regarding cropping and docking, so check the latest legislation in the relevant country.

GROUP TRAITS

GROUPING	TRAITS
Herding dogs	Responsive to training; active; need lots of mental and physical stimulation; loyal; intelligent. Sensitive, so require careful handling.
Hounds	Affectionate; friendly; loyal; independent; difficult to train; can be aloof and suspicious of strangers.
Gundogs	Loyal companions; good-natured; tolerant; keen to please and quick to learn.
Terriers	Lively; curious; tenacious; determined; bossy; vocal; suspicious of strangers; not always child-tolerant.
Guard and Working breeds	Temperament influenced by breeding, upbringing and early environment/socialization; strong-willed; will assert dominance over their owners if not handled appropriately.
Toy breeds	Usually affectionate and friendly; brave watchdogs; can be 'yappy', and 'nippy' if spoilt and poorly trained.

ABOVE To examine the exhibit fully, small dogs are usually judged on a table, so it's important to get your pet used to this.

How do I buy a dog that will win show prizes?

To be certain of prizes, you will have to purchase a dog or puppy that is already a winner in the ring. Be prepared to pay a lot of money for the privilege.

The alternative is to buy a show-quality youngster from a breeder who successfully exhibits and breeds winners. If maturity fulfils the early potential, then the dog could do well provided it is correctly handled, trained and 'produced' for the show ring. You could hire a professional show producer and handler to exhibit your dog for you, which can help enhance your chances in the ring, but of course the dog must be of show standard.

By what standards are dogs judged in the show ring?

Each breed that is recognized by an official kennel club organization has a standard ('blueprint') to which dogs of that breed must conform. With this standard in mind, judges pick out the dogs in the class that best fit that conception. Dogs in a large class of the same breed may appear identical to the inexperienced eye, but to a seasoned judge they are all individuals. The judge will grade them according to the ideal for that breed's standard and place them accordingly.

Where can I see lots of different breeds of dog?

Championship dog shows are the best place to see lots of different breeds under one roof. As well as being able to view the different varieties and colours,

COAT TYPES

Type	Breed example	Characteristics
Smooth and short	Rhodesian Ridgeback	Often thick, sometimes harsh coat, which is quite oily (for waterproofing) in some breeds.
Long	Shih Tzu	Texture varies between fine and silky without much of an undercoat, to harsh with a dense, soft and furry undercoat.
Curly/woolly	Bedlington Terrier	Dense, but usually with minimum 'doggy' odour. Curly coats do not moult, but shed within the existing coat. In the Puli and Komondor, the coat mats (felts) to form long cords.
Wire-haired	Airedale Terrier	Wiry short hair that can look dull if the coat is not maintained correctly. Can be oily for waterproofing.
Double-coated (long- and short-haired dogs)	Rough Collie	Long top layer of coat over a dense undercoat. Prone to matting if not regularly groomed.

you may ask breeders and handlers about the breeds you like the look of. You'll find shows advertised in dog magazines and by breed societies on the internet.

Also invest in a good, up-to-date book on dog breeds, then request details of breeders of the type of dog you prefer from the governing body of that breed.

What are the different canine coat types and how do I recognize them?

There are five different coat types in dogs. If this matters to you then consult the table above for a dog that fits into the category you prefer.

WHAT ARE THE VARIOUS TERMS USED TO DESCRIBE A DOG'S CONFORMATION?

The points of a dog's conformation are shown in the picture below.

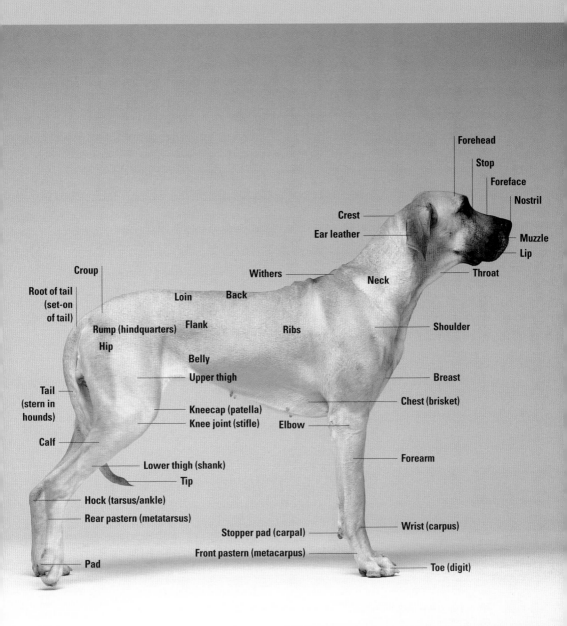

Forehead

Stop

Foreface

Nostril

Crest

Ear leather

Muzzle

Lip

Croup

Withers

Neck

Throat

Root of tail (set-on of tail)

Loin

Back

Rump (hindquarters)

Flank

Ribs

Shoulder

Hip

Belly

Upper thigh

Breast

Tail (stern in hounds)

Kneecap (patella)

Chest (brisket)

Knee joint (stifle)

Elbow

Calf

Forearm

Lower thigh (shank)

Tip

Hock (tarsus/ankle)

Rear pastern (metatarsus)

Stopper pad (carpal)

Wrist (carpus)

Front pastern (metacarpus)

Pad

Toe (digit)

HEAD SHAPES

TYPE	CHARACTERISTICS	BREED EXAMPLE	
Brachycephalic	Compressed skull shape with a short nose.	Pug	
Dolichocephalic	Narrow head shape, with a shallow cranium and long nose.	Borzoi	
Mesocephalic	'Normal' shape, with the width of the skull in proportion to its length.	Golden Retriever	

What do the terms 'brachycephalic', 'dolichocephalic' and 'mesocephalic' mean?

These terms describe the three basic dog head shapes. Mesocephalic describes a medium-sized head, dolichocephalic a long skull and brachycephalic a short, broad skull. The chart above describes the different characteristics and provides breed examples.

Where did the different breeds originate?

Quite often, the country of origin is in the name of the breed. Examples include the Portuguese Water Dog, German Shepherd Dog and Chinese Crested Dog.

However, in other breeds the country of origin is not so obvious – for instance, in the case of the Great Dane, which comes from Germany, not Denmark.

Spitz breeds originated in the Arctic Circle. Some of these dogs were taken to other countries, where they were developed into the various breeds we know today, such as the Japanese Spitz.

A selection of breeds whose country of origin is not apparent are listed in the table on the opposite page.

Is an unusual-coated dog like the Hungarian Puli difficult to look after?

Corded coats are not easy to maintain. The Puli's cords are formed from the soft woolly undercoat intermingling with the

BREED ORIGINS

BREED	COUNTRY OF ORIGIN
Bichon Frise	Tenerife
Schipperke	Belgium
Komondor	Hungary
Rough Collie	Scotland
Clumber Spaniel	France
English Cocker Spaniel	Spain
Labrador Retriever	Newfoundland
American Cocker Spaniel	Spain
Poodle	Germany
Cavalier King Charles Spaniel	Japan
Papillon	Spain
Afghan Hound	Iran (formerly Persia)

coarse top coat. This begins to happen at around 6–9 months of age, when the adult coat starts to come through. At this stage, tufts begin to form close to the skin as the two coats start to entwine, gradually lengthening into cords. From now on, and for the next 12 months or so, it is important not to let the forming cords mat together, otherwise the coat becomes a mass of 'felt', so separate them by gently teasing apart.

How do I groom a corded-coat breed?

There are a number of grooming points to note. The inside of the ears must be kept clear of hair, while the outside growth of cords must be kept separated very gently so as not to tear the delicate skin. The tail also requires much attention so that it does not felt, while hair between the paw pads must be kept trimmed short to prevent it felting and causing discomfort.

The length of the coat will require trimming as necessary. It should never be brushed, but any debris collected during exercise must be removed carefully by hand so as not to disturb the cords. Regular bathing is necessary to keep the skin and coat clean and the cords firm. Drying can take days. The Hungarian Puli and the Komondor are the only breeds with this sort of coat.

LEFT **At 5 years of age the Hungarian Puli's coat has usually grown to its full length and, if it has been properly cared for, is an impressive sight.**

I love dogs but am allergic to them. Would a hairless dog be the answer?

Unfortunately, this won't work. While dog hair is undoubtedly a factor in causing respiratory irritation in those people sensitive to contaminated air, getting a pet without hair won't resolve the problem entirely. The reason for this is that it is actually an allergen (Can d1) present in a dog's saliva and urine, along with microscopic dander (skin flakes), that causes problems for allergy sufferers.

What does the term 'hackney action' mean when used to describe a dog's movement?

Hackney action means high-stepping with the forefeet. The dog lifts them high off the ground in a movement identical to that of a Hackney pony. Breeds that demonstrate this action include the Italian Greyhound, Saluki, Japanese Chin and Miniature Pinscher.

If you have a dog that does not usually have a high-stepping action and suddenly starts to display it, consult your vet. This action is a symptom of dermatomyositis, a hereditary skin/muscle inflammatory disease that most commonly affects Shetland Sheepdogs, Collies and their crosses.

Are there any breeds of dog that do not bark?

The Basenji is the only breed of domestic dog that does not bark in the accepted sense. However, this does not mean that it is quiet – in fact, it can be quite the opposite. Instead of barking, it makes a peculiar sound called 'yodelling', along with a repertoire of other unique noises such as chortling, crowing, wolf-like howling and leopard-like growling, 'burrs' and 'roos'.

We don't want a 'yappy' dog. Which breeds should we avoid?

The smaller Spitz breeds have a tendency to yap (a sharp, shrill bark), as do many terriers and guarding breeds. Bear in mind that any dog will bark to sound an alarm to its pack (human or animal), or to warn off what it perceives as a threat. With training, dogs can be taught not to bark when inappropriate or for prolonged periods, and this is something all dog owners should do.

LEFT The ballerina-like, high-stepping, Italian Greyhound is prized for its slender elegance.

How can I tell how big a non-pedigree puppy from a rescue centre will grow?

If you don't know what size the parents were, this can be very difficult to judge. However, generally the size of the feet will provide a fairly rough guide – large dogs tend to have correspondingly large feet. A puppy that will grow into a large dog tends to be of substantial build and frame, and have big paws and joints in relation to its size.

What are the options for canine identification (ID)?

A tag on the collar bearing the owner's contact details is the traditional method. Unfortunately, these are easily lost or removed. A more permanent way of proving identification is by having a microchip bearing ID details implanted in the animal. Tattooing is another permanent means of ID, whereby a

ABOVE The timbre of smaller dogs' barking can prove very irritating if prolonged. Pomeranians, West Highland White Terriers and Yorkshire Terriers can be some of the worst culprits.

unique code number is imprinted on a dog's inner ear leather, lip, stomach or inner thigh.

Take close-up colour photographs of your dog from all angles every year of its life for visual ID, and note down any unusual markings, characteristics and physical aspects that can help prove your dog's identity.

Which type of permanent ID marking is the best?

There are advantages and disadvantages to both microchips and tattoos. It is up to you to decide which would be most appropriate for your dog. A permanently marked dog is, however, preferable to an unmarked one.

MICROCHIP OR TATTOO?

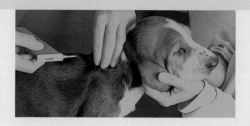

ABOVE Microchips are usually inserted in the scruff of the neck via a special needle.

MICROCHIP

Pros

- Enhances the chances of a lost dog being returned safely.

- Relatively painless.

- Invisible.

- Permanent.

Cons

- Proof of ownership. A special, compatible, scanner is required to read the microchip, which may not be available when needed, so there is no guarantee the dog will be returned to its owner.

- There is no outwardly obvious sign that the dog is ID-marked (unless it wears a warning collar tag), so no deterrent against theft.

- In some cases, chips have been known to move under the skin, so are not evident when the dog is scanned.

- It is not known whether the chips will create any long-term health problems.

- Some chips have proved not to be of the required standard for pet passport requirements, necessitating re-chipping of the dog by an approved source.

- Microchip companies who hold the database can cease trading, leaving no tracing service.

TATTOO

Pros

After collar tagging, tattooing is the most widely used tried-and-tested form of canine ID.

- Permanent.

- Relatively painless.

- Cosmetically acceptable.

- Instantly traceable.

- Proof of ownership/breeding.

- Visually obvious so deters thieves.

Cons

- Home DIY kits can prove disastrous, in terms of both discomfort for the dog and botched results.

- There have been reports of tattoos being tampered with, and tattooed areas of skin being removed by thieves.

- If inexpertly done at too young an age, tattoos can stretch and become disfigured with age.

- Tattooing companies who hold the database can cease trading, leaving no tracing service.

JAW ALIGNMENTS

TYPE	CHARACTERISTICS
Good mouth (scissor bite)	An even (scissor) bite, in which the top and bottom jaws are aligned and the upper incisors just overlap the lower when the jaw is closed.
Overshot mouth (brachygnathism)	The upper jaw is longer than the lower, with the lower row of teeth behind the uppers when the mouth is shut.
Undershot mouth (prognathism)	The lower jaw is longer than the upper, with the lower incisors lying in front of the uppers when the jaw is closed.

What is meant by a 'good mouth', 'undershot' and 'overshot'?

These terms describe the alignment of a dog's top and bottom jaws. This affects the alignment of the two sets of teeth: a 'good mouth' minimizes dental and eating problems, and ensures effective mastication and therefore utilization of food. 'Malocclusion' is the term used for incorrect jaw structure.

We are a disabled couple. Which breeds are ideal indoor pets that do not need much exercise?

In your case, consider a Toy breed. Many of these dogs will get sufficient mental and physical exercise by running around the house, and you'll have plenty of scope for indoor games and training. The latter is important in order to teach your pet to be obedient, so as not to cause problems with your limited mobility.

Low coat-maintenance breeds include the Dachshund, Pug, Chihuahua and Whippet. If you are able to cope with long coats, then consider the Bolognese, Maltese, Havanese, Pomeranian, Papillon, Pekinese, Japanese Chin, King Charles or Cavalier King Charles Spaniel.

Are there any breeds that will live happily outdoors?

Most breeds will live outdoors provided they are accustomed and acclimatized to it. Dogs that live outside will need a suitable-sized, weatherproof kennel that is cool in summer and warm in winter. This should lead into a spacious, secure pen in which the dog can exercise and toilet, so requires a suitable surface.

If the dog is a thin-skinned or thin-coated breed, then it will need a heat source during cold weather, such as infra-red lamps or a bed warmer, plus a well-fitting dog coat. Otherwise, the dog will lose condition and be extremely miserable. A bed with plenty of warm bedding is essential.

BELOW The Border Collie tends to be the best at agility and flyball. Border Collie crosses are also good choices.

Which breeds would be most suitable for flyball and agility activities?

Agile, fast and light breeds tend to be most successful. However, most dogs will enjoy having a go, so if you want to do these activities for fun and mutual enjoyment rather than competing, choose whichever breed appeals to you.

Flyball consists of a box-like piece of equipment that throws out a ball when the dog steps on a 'pedal', for the dog to catch and take back to its handler. Agility comprises a course of jumps and other obstacles for the dog to negotiate. Bear in mind that slower, 'chunky' breeds are

limited in the height they can jump and the speed at which they can negotiate obstacles, but that won't stop them having fun over a course they can manage comfortably.

Are there any breeds named after characteristics they display, or people who founded the breed?

There are lots of examples of both. The Papillon (French for butterfly), for instance, was named for its butterfly-shaped ears, while the King Charles and Cavalier King Charles Spaniels were named after the English King Charles II, who popularized the breeds.

Dandie Dinmonts are said to be named after a character in the English novelist Sir Walter Scott's book *Guy Mannering*, and the Labradoodle is a derivative of the cross between a Labrador and a Poodle.

BELOW LEFT It is thought that Boxers got their name from their characteristic of fighting and playing with their forepaws.

BELOW The Keeshond is named after the Dutch patriot Kees de Gyselaer, the owner of an early example of the breed.

Do any breeds suffer more than others from particular health problems?

The majority of pedigree breeds (particularly of show type) suffer from genetic weaknesses, with some worse than others. Ear infections, hip, knee and elbow dysplasia (joint deformity), eye and liver defects, malocclusion (jaw/teeth deformity), atopy (allergy/hyper-sensitivity), respiratory and pulmonary (heart/lung) diseases, and skin and muscle ailments are the most commonly seen problems.

Examples include the Bulldog, whose skull conformation is so abnormal that it causes respiratory distress so severe that there have been veterinary calls for the breed to be banned in its current form. Joint problems and bloat are seen in large and giant breeds, hip dysplasia in sporting, working and gundogs, and heart and eye defects in Cavalier King Charles Spaniels.

What is the reason for these ailments and can they be eliminated?

Over the years, inbreeding to fix and maintain a standard has led to inherent genetic weaknesses within the majority of pedigree breeds. Responsible breeders today are doing their best to eliminate these weaknesses by health screening their breeding stock and using only those animals that are sound and are derived from healthy forebears. It pays to be aware of these weaknesses.

Before buying a puppy, take time to research preferred breeds carefully to check what, if any, ailments they are prone to. Having done this, you will be aware of what to watch out for, and what to ask breeders regarding health screening of the parents before they were bred from.

What does the term 'hip scoring' mean?

Hip dysplasia is a condition where the hip joint has not developed normally. Hip scoring is done to ascertain how well constructed a dog's hips are. X-rays are taken of the hips and submitted to experts, who give scores to each hip reflecting the depth of the socket, the shape of the structures, and how well the 'ball and socket' joint fits together. The lower the score, the better the hips.

Most breeds prone to the condition have an average hip score; only those animals with a lower than average score should be bred from (both dogs and bitches), to help prevent deformed hips in their offspring.

Do Poodles have to have 'show ring' clips?

While the awesome Lion Trim – complete with long 'mane' and pompoms on legs and tail – looks superb, it is not necessary to have your Poodle trimmed like this. In fact, there are a variety of coat styles for Poodles and, just like choosing a hair style for yourself, you can ask a canine beautician to show you various styles suitable for the Poodle's shape, conformation and woolly coat. Some people choose not to have pompoms (except on the tail tip) – which is called the Puppy Trim – while others like the coat short all over.

Why are some dogs aggressive?

Given the wrong kind of treatment and handling, any dog can be aggressive towards people. This is true no matter how docile and kindly the breed is normally. In these cases, such behaviour simply demonstrates what the dog regards as self-preservation.

Some dogs are aggressive towards others of their kind, and other animals too. This is because either they have not been socialized properly at an appropriate age, and/or they have a strong inbred fight or chase/dispatch instinct.

Correct, sensible handling from an early age usually negates problems, but there are some breeds that only experienced handlers should consider owning, and such dogs are not advised if there are children in the household (see page 42).

I don't want a dog that is unpredictable towards children and other dogs. Which breeds should I avoid?

The chart on page 42 lists the main breeds to avoid. Remember that many sighthounds, such as Greyhounds, are likely to chase after other animals (especially small, furry ones), and kill them if they get the chance, unless they have been brought up with them. Similarly, some scenthounds are not suited to life as family pets due to their strong hunting instincts and sometimes powerful build, which is not a good combination when there are children and other pets in the household. It pays to research thoroughly the breed you are interested in before buying a puppy, or taking on an adult.

LEFT Despite having the reputation of a 'glamour dog', Poodles are actually tough all-rounders that make fantastic family pets.

AGGRESSIVE BREEDS

BREEDS UNSUITABLE AS FAMILY PETS	BREEDS TYPICALLY AGGRESSIVE TOWARDS OTHER DOGS (including those in the left-hand column)
Pit Bull Terrier (American Staffordshire Terrier)	English Bull Terrier
	Alaskan Malamute
Japanese Fighting Dog (Tosa Inu)	Kerry Blue Terrier
Neopolitan Mastiff	Sealyham
Dogo Argentino	Irish Terrier
Fila Brasileiro	Bulldog
Pyrenean Mastiff	Shar Pei
Spanish Mastiff	Bouvier des Flandres
German Hunt Terrier	German Shepherd Dog
Karelian Bear Dog	Briard
Chow Chow	Japanese Akita

Any cross-breeds of the above, or crosses between these and other breeds having strong guarding/fighting instincts.

NOTE It is usually the males that can be aggressive towards other dogs when they have not been adequately socialized with them from puppyhood.

Which dogs are the most difficult to train?

Both sighthounds and scenthounds need a lot of patience while training. These dogs tend to be slow at processing information, and both can be difficult to recall if they see or scent something they find interesting!

Giant breeds are slow thinkers and require a great deal of patience too, while terriers can be stubborn and self-willed. Spitz breeds are intelligent but have an independent temperament.

Sporting, herding and guarding breeds tend to be the most easily trained, but they do not take kindly to heavy-handed training methods.

Is it better to get a puppy or an adult dog?

Your lifestyle and circumstances must be taken into account here. Being babies, puppies are time-consuming and labour intensive, while an older dog is more likely to be clean in the house, have been trained in the basics of obedience, and potentially socialized with people and other animals.

Puppies are easier to integrate into the family and socialize, while the characteristics of an older dog will be easier to ascertain, plus any difficult or undesirable traits will be apparent.

Bear in mind that if there are young children in the house they will need a good deal of supervision around the animal, whether you acquire a pup or an adult dog.

BELOW Afghan Hounds, though beautiful, are not renowned for being quick on the uptake as far as obedience training is concerned.

2

Caring for your puppy

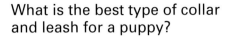

Before I get a puppy, what equipment will I need?

The basic equipment you will need should include the following:

- Collar of broad nylon or leather and a leash, preferably adjustable.
- Food bowl and water bowl – ceramic or stainless steel are the most hygienic and durable.
- Bed – to save money, choose one that will accommodate your pet when he is fully grown. A strong cardboard box with one side cut down is ideal as a first bed, especially for teething pups.
- Bedding – fleece bedding made specially for dogs' beds is ideal. Old duvets and blankets are also suitable.
- Grooming tools. (For further information, see page 47).
- Toys suitable for puppies (see pages 47–48).
- Puppy food.

What is the best type of collar and leash for a puppy?

A broad nylon or leather collar is the most comfortable and kindest for a puppy. Choose a three-in-one training leash, which can be adjusted to three different lengths depending on the situation or training exercise. Ensure that neither collar nor leash is too heavy for the size of the puppy, and that the collar is of a suitable width.

As your puppy will grow rapidly, you need to ensure that the collar does not become too tight, so check it every few days. You should be able to get two or three fingers underneath it. If it is too loose it will slip off, or the puppy may get a leg caught up in it while scratching or playing. If it is too tight it will cause discomfort, particularly when the puppy is eating and drinking, and it may rub the skin.

LEFT AND BELOW Buying the equipment you need represents a sizeable outlay initially, but most of it should last for quite some time.

What equipment do I need to groom my puppy?

This depends on your puppy's coat type. Suitable equipment for each type is shown in the table below.

A spray-on protein finishing spray is useful to help keep the coat shiny and tangle-free, while anti-static spray helps to keep fine, silky coats manageable while grooming. You will need straight, round-tipped scissors for trimming excess foot hair. For advice on nail-trimming, see page 63.

What sort of toys are most suitable for a puppy?

Choose toys appropriate for the size of your puppy. Avoid small balls that could get stuck in the throat, or flimsy plastic or fabric toys that could easily be shredded

ABOVE Puppies' coats are fine and their skin tender, so be extremely gentle while grooming.

GROOMING EQUIPMENT

COAT TYPE	SUITABLE EQUIPMENT
Short, smooth-coated dogs	Rubber slicker or rubber brush. Lint-free duster for a final polish.
Long-hairs	Firm, long-bristled brush with space between the bristles, or slicker brush. Wide-toothed comb to help tease out tangles. Hair clips are useful to separate sections of hair.
Wire-hairs	Fine-toothed comb or terrier pad.
Double coats	Slicker brush and wide-toothed comb.
Curly/woolly coats	Slicker brush and wide-toothed comb.

and swallowed by teething/curious puppies. Sticks are unsuitable, as are stones – both can cause serious injury.

Only allow play toys under supervision so that if he gets into trouble someone is there to help him out. Tough 'indestructible' toys, such as genuine Kongs or Nylabones, are fine for unsupervised play and are especially good for teething puppies.

Is it all right to give a puppy an old shoe or slipper to play with?

These items can provide entertainment for a puppy but are not ideal. The puppy may not differentiate between your unwanted footwear and your best pair of shoes, and this could become a problem that is difficult to cure.

The same principle is applied to clothing: it may seem a good idea to use an old coat as a tug toy, but the puppy may well then view all your items of clothing as such.

What's the most suitable diet for a puppy?

Reputable breeders are usually happy to supply a diet sheet when puppies go to new homes. This will give advice on what food the puppy is receiving, how much and when. Adhere to this recommended diet wherever possible,

BELOW Choose a selection of toys to satisfy your puppy's natural instincts to chase, pounce, stalk, grab, shake, bite and 'kill'.

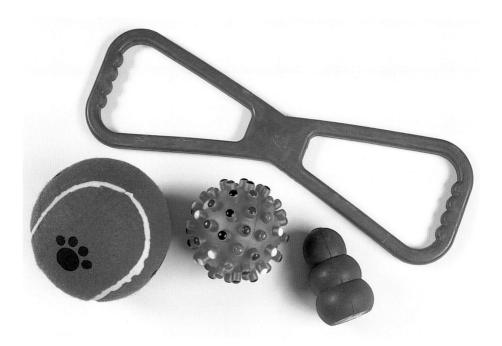

ABOVE **Do not overfeed puppies, otherwise obesity and/or too quick a growth rate will occur, both of which are detrimental to health.**

How many meals should a puppy have, with how much food in each meal?

The number of meals per day at different ages is shown in the table below. Quantities of food to give depend on the breed and size, and are indicated on the packets of good-quality puppy food. However, these are only approximate, so increase or decrease the suggested amounts as required, depending on your puppy's weight and growth rate.

If in doubt as to the type and amount of food to feed, ask your vet for advice.

to help avoid your puppy suffering a tummy upset. If you change the diet, then do so over a period of days, gradually adding the new food and reducing the old.

Proprietary brands of food specially formulated for puppies are easy to feed, and contain all the nutrients for growing pups in a form that is easy for them to digest and utilize.

Is it better to feed a home-made diet or a commercial dog food?

With puppies, a good-quality commercially prepared food is preferable. This is especially true when the food is aimed at particular breeds (such as large and giant breeds), as it will contain all the ingredients and nutrients a young dog needs for healthy, normal

FEEDING PUPPIES

AGE	NUMBER OF MEALS
Weaning to 20 weeks	Three meals daily, plus baby or puppy formula milk at night.
20 to 30 weeks	Three meals daily.
30 weeks to 9 months	Two meals daily (depending on breed/growth rate).
Over 9 months	One to two meals daily.

growth and development. Trying to recreate such a diet yourself would be extremely difficult.

Advocates of natural canine diets (fresh foods minus artificial ingredients) maintain that raising healthy puppies is perfectly possible, provided guidelines are adhered to. You will find these in books about providing a natural, balanced canine diet. Bear in mind that dogs have different nutritional needs at different stages of their lives.

Which commercial dog foods are most suitable for puppies?

There are many brands available, so choosing can be difficult. However, it is recommended that you choose a puppy food bearing a 'famous name', and particularly one that has minimal artificial ingredients, especially colourings.

Well-known dog food manufacturers generally have a proven track record in canine nutrition. Their teams of nutritional experts spend considerable time formulating and testing preparations to ensure that they produce the best possible balanced diet for the type, size and age of dog at which it is aimed.

Can puppies have bones to chew?

Allowing your puppy to gnaw on a large, raw, meaty marrowbone will help keep his teeth and gums in good order. Big cooked or sterilized bones bought from pet stores are also fine, but remove them

when they begin to break up to avoid the puppy swallowing sharp bone slivers. Dispose of bones when they begin to go 'off' to avoid digestive upsets.

Don't give your puppy poultry bones as these break easily and splinter, causing injuries to the mouth and stomach if swallowed. Avoid giving small, cooked bones, such as ribs or chops.

Meat-impregnated nylon bones are good for promoting oral health, but again throw them away once they start to break up.

BELOW Large hide bones provide entertainment and help maintain good oral hygiene, but never leave a puppy unattended with one in case of choking.

How much water do I need to give a puppy to drink?

The bigger the dog, the more water he will need to drink daily to remain healthy. A bowl that holds 1–2 litres (2–4½ pints) is usually sufficient for most breeds. Replace the water once or twice a day to ensure it is clean.

Note how much your puppy usually drinks per day by measuring it, so that you know when he isn't drinking normally and are alerted to possible health problems. Do this over a period of a week during both hot and cold weather in order to work out the average amounts per day for both. For advice on bowl hygiene, see page 88.

Which is better for my puppy, tap or bottled water?

Tap water is absolutely fine. You do not need to go to the expense of providing bottled water. It is thought that some dogs prone to bladder stones can have their problem exacerbated by mineral-rich bottled water, or the minerals in extremely hard tap water. In the latter case, if you are worried about this you can opt for soft bottled water without added minerals.

BELOW Ensure your puppy always has access to clean, fresh water. Put the water in a wide-topped bowl that will prove hard for him to knock over.

How much daily care and time does a new puppy need from his owner?

Young pups require as much care and supervision as young children. If you want a healthy, sociable, well-mannered pet that is clean and non-destructive in the house, then you need to put in the initial groundwork while he is young. This means being at home with the puppy for most of the time for the first week or two in order to feed, exercise, toilet train and socialize with him, as well as to carry out basic 'nursery' training.

If you work you should book time off, to ensure your puppy's needs are catered for. Be in no doubt: puppies are hard work, and patience and time will be needed in the first year of ownership.

What is the best way to enclose my garden to make it escape-proof?

This is important, as dogs that are able to escape pose a risk to themselves and others. The cheapest option is to erect an impenetrable fence; if you can afford it, have a wall built. Stout boarding or chain link/heavy-duty small-gauge stock netting is ideal, the bottom edges being buried so that your puppy cannot tunnel or wriggle under the fence. It needs to be high enough so that he cannot jump out and other dogs cannot jump in. Gates must also be made escape-proof.

RIGHT If there's a gap in your fence, your puppy is sure to find it and escape.

How often should I clean my puppy's bed, bedding and toys?

Wash beds and bedding weekly to keep both clean and sweet-smelling. Toys should also receive a weekly scrub to remove dirt and dried-on saliva. Stagger toy washing so that your puppy always has something to play with.

Use a mild non-biological soap to wash bedding and toys, and a mild diluted disinfectant for the bed. Make sure bedding and toys are rinsed thoroughly to remove all traces of soap, otherwise your pup is likely to end up scratching at irritated skin and foaming at the mouth!

Should I bath my puppy? If so, how often and with what?

It is a good idea to get a puppy used to having baths. This is because it's physically difficult to bath an adult dog who isn't used to and comfortable with

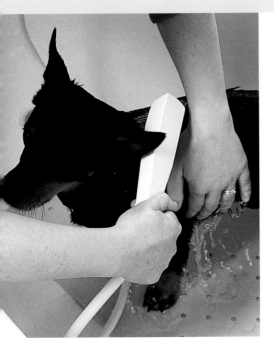

LEFT Put a rubber bath mat in the sink or bath to provide a firm footing so that the puppy feels safe.

uncomfortable). Ensure you work the shampoo right down to the skin, then rinse all shampoo and conditioner out of the puppy's coat to prevent skin irritation later. Some conditioners are designed to be left in the coat.

How often do puppies need grooming?

This depends on the puppy's coat type. The requirements for various coat types are shown in the table below.

When grooming, pay particular attention to behind the ears, inside the elbow crease, between the legs, under the tail and the tail itself, as these are all areas prone to matting. Gently handle the puppy's paws, ears, tail and legs, and inspect his mouth, to get him used to these grooming procedures before he reaches adulthood.

the procedure. Generally, a pup will only need a bath if he gets very dirty or smelly; otherwise, once every 2–3 months is sufficient. Use only dog shampoos and coat conditioners.

The water temperature should be tepid/warm (use the elbow test to make sure it isn't too hot and therefore

GROOMING

COAT TYPE	GROOMING REGIME
Short	Brush weekly.
Long and double	Groom daily to prevent tangles and matting.
Curly and woolly	Groom every other day. Have the coat trimmed professionally every 4–8 weeks.
Wire-haired	Groom every day. Have the coat professionally hand-stripped (coat removed by hand, not brush or clippers) three or four times a year.

HOW CAN I TELL IF A PUPPY IS HEALTHY?

Signs to look for are detailed below.

A healthy puppy

Alert, curious demeanour; bright, clear eyes; clean nose (a slight clear wetness is normal); glossy, clean coat; clean, supple skin free from scurf and parasites; clean ears that do not smell (test the hearing by making a sound out of the puppy's field of vision and see if it registers); clean anal area; no lumps or bumps (especially on the navel); clean teeth and pink gums; normal body weight; flat abdomen (unless the puppy has recently eaten); quiet, even breathing; free and easy movement.

An unhealthy puppy

Subdued, frightened or miserable demeanour; cloudy or weepy eyes (pupils widely dilated in bright light can indicate blindness); dirty, smelly ears; scurfy, flaking or scabby skin with evidence of parasite infestation; open sores; constant scratching (indicated by the action or by red, inflamed areas on the skin); soiled anal area (with evidence of diarrhoea); umbilical hernia; swollen abdomen (can indicate worms); dirty and unkempt or dull and 'staring' coat; stiff or lame movement; constant whining.

At what age is a puppy ready to leave his mother and go to a new home?

Puppies are normally weaned by the age of 6 weeks. At this age a puppy is able to live independently of its mother as regards food, but it still needs the comfort and security of her and its siblings for another week or so to hone its socialization skills within the family environment. Between the ages of 6 and 7 weeks is the period when these vital skills are learnt.

At 8 weeks a puppy is usually mentally and physically able to cope well with being separated from his canine family and adapting to a new home. Any earlier than this and his socialization abilities may be compromised.

Is it better to get two puppies from a litter, to avoid loneliness?

There are probably more disadvantages than advantages to this. While you fondly imagine that two dogs will provide company for each other when you are not there, dogs don't think in the same way as humans. Another dog means competition for food and attention, so you may well end up with two warring siblings as they get older. If you do get two from the same litter, choose one of each sex to reduce friction.

Consider whether you have the space for and can afford two dogs. Once the novelty of cute puppyhood has worn off, you may find you have taken on more than you can handle. Bear in mind also that two dogs may bond more closely with each other than with you.

Will a puppy need any special care when he arrives at his new home?

On arrival, take your puppy into the garden so that he can relieve himself. Praise him lavishly when he does so. Then allow him to investigate his new home at leisure.

Show your puppy where his bed/crate is situated, so that he knows where to go to sleep or take time out when he feels the need. Puppies sleep a lot, so make sure he is not disturbed when he is resting; a tired puppy is more likely to become snappy and 'unreasonable'.

Show him also where his food and water bowls are and provide him with toys (see pages 47–48).

RIGHT Although it's tempting to make a fuss of a new puppy, wait until he has settled down before doing so.

What is the best way to transport a puppy to his new home?

By far the best option is to buy, rent or borrow a suitable-sized dog crate. This can be used to transport your puppy in the car. With a crate, the driver is reassured that the puppy is safely enclosed, so is better able to concentrate on driving. Moreover, in the event of an accident, the puppy will (hopefully) be kept safely enclosed in the crate.

Never put a puppy in the boot of the car, as he may be traumatized by the experience or even suffocate.

Should I let my puppy out of the crate or feed/water him on the journey home?

On a long journey, take a rest stop after 2 hours. You can offer a drink of water, but it's wise not to let him out of the crate in case he escapes.

It's better not to feed the puppy during the journey, or for a couple of hours prior to it, as travelling on a full stomach could cause car-sickness. A small treat is fine.

BELOW Place the crate in the back of an estate car or on the back seat of a saloon (use a seatbelt to secure it), so that movement will be minimal.

How can I keep travel stress to a minimum when bringing a puppy home?

A few days before you intend to bring your new puppy home, take some bedding to the breeder. Ask them to transfer the scent of the puppy's mother and littermates onto it (by rubbing it over them).

On collection, put the bedding in the travel crate, place the pup inside and give him a treat, along with praise, so that he views the crate as a nice place to be. As it will smell familiar, he shouldn't be too bothered by his new surroundings.

Once you get home, transfer the bedding into the puppy's bed so that this will smell like 'home', so providing both mental and physical comfort.

What will make the journey more pleasant for the puppy?

Drive carefully and smoothly so that the puppy is not thrown and bounced around in his crate. If your puppy seems upset by travelling, try giving him a Kong toy stuffed with cheese paste or a flavoured synthetic chew toy (Nylabone or similar) that will not break or split (see page 48), to help keep him happily and safely occupied during the journey. Covering the crate with a blanket can help to keep the puppy calm and quiet.

RIGHT **A puppy that is allowed to manipulate his owner may turn into an adult that dominates the human members of the household, to the point of turning nasty when denied what he wants.**

There must be sufficient ventilation in the car and the temperature should be neither too warm nor too cold, so that the puppy remains comfortable.

Will 'spoiling' a new puppy help him settle in quicker and bond better with his owner?

It's important not to pander to your new puppy's every whim. If you do, he will learn that pestering you when he wants something – be it food, attention, or the most comfortable chair all to himself – gets the result he wants.

Be gentle with him and sympathetic to his needs, but also firm in what you will and won't allow him to do. Fair, firm and consistent handling is more effective than 'spoiling'.

How should I treat a puppy that cries constantly at night?

So that the pup feels more secure and you get an undisturbed night's sleep, try the following:
● Have the puppy in a crate in your bedroom close to your bed. A flavoured chew toy will help to keep him occupied.
● The following night, move the crate further away from the bed, moving further each night until outside the bedroom with the door shut. You may get some whimpering but unless it persists, ignore it.
● When you feel the time is right – usually after the first week, when the puppy has settled down and feels more at home – move his crate downstairs.

When should my puppy start to wear a collar?

Let him settle into his new home for a day or two, then put a collar on him. The sooner he learns to accept it, the better. Put it on for short periods at first, praising him lavishly, then distract him with a game or a stuffed activity toy. By doing this, he'll view wearing the collar as a pleasant experience. Do not leave the collar on when you are not there, in case he gets caught up on something.

Gradually extend the length of time that the puppy wears the collar, until he's happy wearing it permanently. You should still remove the collar for safety reasons when he's left on his own.

How do I teach my puppy his name?

This is really easy. Simply crouch down in front of your puppy, open your arms wide (an inviting gesture) and call his name. When he comes to you – as he is sure to, out of curiosity – give him a food treat and/or lots of fuss. He will soon come to recognize his name – probably within days – as he associates the sound of it with nice things.

When should I start training my puppy?

Straight away is the simple answer. However, this does not involve anything intense: simply start as you mean to go on as regards manners and obedience. Begin with toilet training (see page 64), and teaching him his name and to come to you when you call him (see above).

Move on to collar and leash training (see this page and the opposite page), and then progress by encouraging him not to jump on furniture or chew your hands or clothing. When he relieves himself outside, praise him. When he lies quietly without pestering, reward him. Reward desirable behaviour, ignore undesirable behaviour and he'll soon get the message.

Channel games into what will later become recall and retrieve exercises. Once he's been vaccinated, take him to puppy socialization classes.

When can leash training begin?

You can do this once your puppy knows his name and is used to wearing a collar. Attach a short, light leash to it and let him drag it around under supervision, while being praised and rewarded.

BELOW LEFT Teaching your puppy his name is quick and easy.

BELOW If the puppy is reluctant to follow, let him mouth a toy or treat, then start moving away from him again and call his name – this time he'll probably get the idea and follow.

Once he's accustomed to this, clip on the leash proper, hold it in one hand while holding a treat or toy in the other, and slowly walk backwards, calling his name and enticing him to accompany you with the treat or toy. Keep the leash slack – never pull on it – and reward him when he follows you.

How soon after I get him can I take my puppy for walks?

Keep him away from other dogs until he is fully vaccinated (see below). It is wise to exercise him only in your enclosed garden or yard until he is protected against canine diseases. You will also have to train your puppy to the collar and leash before you can take him out, and make sure he'll come back to you when you call him.

Be careful not to expect too much of your puppy too soon and expose him to situations he cannot cope with, as this will create a nervous individual. It is better to gradually introduce him to sights and sounds outside the safe and familiar confines of your home, such as people, vehicles and other dogs.

Which vaccinations will my puppy require to help safeguard his health?

It is a wise precaution to have your puppy inoculated against canine diseases that can be contagious and/or fatal. Puppies can be vaccinated as early as 6 weeks old, but 8 weeks is preferable as

ABOVE Wait until your puppy has been given all his injections and been trained to the collar and leash before taking him outside the confines of your garden.

the vaccine is more effective; they will need two injections of multiple vaccines 2–4 weeks apart. The second injection cannot be given before the puppy is 10 weeks old.

The inoculations comprise vaccines that protect against canine distemper (D), canine adenovirus (types 1 [CAV 1] and 2 [CAV-2], both of which cause canine infectious hepatitis and can sometimes be involved in the infectious tracheobronchitis [kennel cough] syndrome).

In certain countries, vaccinations for rabies are also given routinely. Dogs must be vaccinated in order to re-enter the country after travelling abroad.

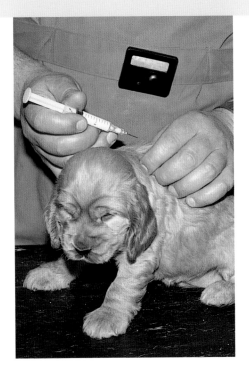

Can humans catch diseases from dogs?

Any disease which can be transmitted to humans from animals is called a zoonosis. Canine zoonoses that affect humans are caused by viruses, bacteria and parasites. Some have serious health implications, while others are minor irritations. These are some of the most common diseases that can be transferred to humans:

Parasitic Toxocara canis is the common roundworm of dogs. Worm eggs are passed out in the dog's faeces and people can become infected if their hands or food come into contact with dog faeces which is subsequently ingested. The infection is known as toxocariasis. The worm eggs hatch out and migrate through body tissues; in rare cases they can invade the eye causing blindness (more usually in children). Most infections are harmless if the person concerned has sufficient immunity (expectant mothers included). Good hygiene measures comprising washing hands after handling dogs, cleaning up dog faeces and regular de-worming of dogs are important control measures.

Bacterial Weil's Disease (Leptospirosis) is the result of an infection with an organism called Leptospira of which there are many sub-types. Infected dogs may spread the disease to humans; the dog's urine is particularly heavily contaminated with the organism. It is a serious illness causing 'flu-like symptoms.

Viral Rabies is a fatal disease contracted by being bitten by a rabid dog. There is no cure and treatment is aimed at trying to boost immunity to the virus by vaccinating the victim immediately after they have been exposed to a rabid dog. Vaccination of pet dogs is a routine and worthwhile preventative measure in areas where rabies occurs.

Fungal Ringworm is a skin infection caused by many species of fungus and all mammals are susceptible to it to variable degrees. Although the condition is relatively uncommon in dogs, infected dogs will be a source of infection for people. It causes an itchy skin rash that is readily treatable. Children are more susceptible to it than adults. In severe cases it can leave the skin marked.

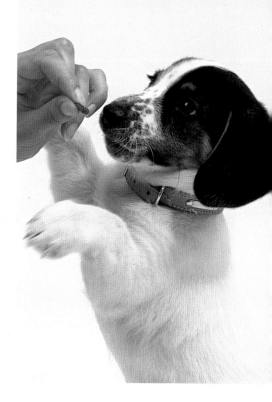

RIGHT Keep play-exercise sessions short, calm and non-strenuous to avoid overtaxing your puppy's immature body.

What should I do if I think my puppy is unwell?

Start recognizing your puppy's normal behaviour as soon as you get him. Then you will know when all is not well. Note any unusual behaviour, altered appetite or demeanour, distressed whining, increased or decreased thirst, straining on defecation or urination, vomiting or diarrhoea. You will be able to inform your vet of the symptoms.

Puppies with digestive upsets can soon become dehydrated, as the body loses moisture and essential salts and sugars (electrolytes), so it is imperative they are seen by a vet within a couple of hours if an ailment has not cleared up. If the condition worsens during this time, consult a vet sooner.

Maintain your puppy's natural sleep-play pattern and let him retire when he wants to, otherwise his body and mind will be stressed.

How much exercise does a puppy need?

Play exercise is a high priority for puppies, along with sleeping and eating. Short, energetic bursts of play are interspersed with meals and longer bouts of sleeping. Because they are so lively when awake, it's tempting to sustain play, but such activity in excess can have a detrimental effect on soft, growing bones and joints – especially in large and giant breeds – and can cause problems in later life.

Is it all right to let our puppy play 'rough and tumble' with the children?

While this seems great fun initially, it is all too easy for such play to get out of hand. The puppy grows bigger and the playful mouthing becomes full-blown nips and bites that really hurt as the dog becomes overexcited. It's not at all funny when a fully grown dog hurls himself on a person in anticipation of a 'wrestle', and can actually prove frightening if the 'game'

becomes a case of asserting dominance, as can easily happen – especially where male dogs are concerned.

ABOVE Make sure children do not encourage the puppy to play roughly, as this usually ends in tears.

Our puppy's nails are very sharp – how can we remedy this?

Trimming your puppy's nail tips will prevent them getting too sharp. It also accustoms him to the procedure before he gets too big to object. It is best to have your vet (or veterinary nurse) or a local canine beautician do this for you.

Inside each nail is a 'quick' – a tiny vein that appears pink in white nails, but is invisible in dark ones. If it is nicked during trimming, this will prove extremely painful for the puppy; it will also bleed profusely.

To reduce the risk of this happening, this procedure is best left to experts. As the pup matures, exercise on hard surfaces will wear down his nails naturally.

How should I introduce our new puppy to our other pets?

Before introductions, transfer scent from the other pets onto your pup's bedding, and vice versa. Do this by swapping a piece of used bedding so that they learn to recognize each other's scent.

Pen the puppy before introducing other resident pets (dogs and cats), so that they can see and sniff each other without risk of damaging contact. You can then gauge how soon you can safely let the pup out to mingle with them. Don't be upset if the other pets' reaction is not welcoming, as it takes time for them to accept another into their environment. However, a pecking order should soon be established with the minimum of fuss.

When should I start house-training my puppy?

Dogs are not naturally clean in the house, so you have to train them. When you get your puppy, take him outside to empty his bowels/bladder many times during the day and evening – usually after eating, on waking and after playing.

You'll soon get to know when he wants to go, as he will be distracted and sniff the floor, hunting for a suitable place.

Accept that your puppy will have the occasional accident, so keep him in areas (especially at night) where his mess can be cleaned up easily, until he's fully house-trained.

Can you teach a puppy to use an indoor tray or a specific toileting area outside?

You certainly can. Define an area outside by laying rope to mark it off, or build a specific toileting place by laying sharp sand (builders' sand stains the puppy's coat) or shredded bark on the surface.

BELOW Discourage the pup from harassing caged pets by distracting him with a toy or game so that he loses interest, then reward him.

needs to toilet – be prepared to wait a while. When he performs, praise him lavishly so that he knows his actions in that place are desirable. He'll quickly work out that going outside to toilet is rewarded and he'll learn to do so as a matter of course when nature calls. Use the same procedure for tray training.

How do I teach my puppy to sit and stay on command?

Puppies do not have a prolonged attention span and tire quickly, so keep training sessions short. Five or ten minutes a day is plenty, and it is best if you can turn the training into a game. By doing this, your puppy is more likely to be responsive to your requirements.

Whenever he sits unprompted by you, reward him. Then put the command 'sit' to the action and reward him with a treat. He will soon realize that 'sit' is rewarding and will start responding to the prompted spoken command. Follow the same principle with the 'stay' exercise.

For further information on teaching sit and stay, see pages 146–148.

How should I reward my puppy when he behaves well and obeys me?

Puppies are very motivated by food, so treats are useful training aids and rewards, as are toys, attention and vocal praise. Cut all food treats into tiny pieces so they go further without posing a weight-gain problem.

ABOVE Teaching a puppy to use a specific toileting place is easy when you know how.

The practicality of having an inside toilet tray depends on the size and sex of the dog. It would not be feasible with anything other than a small pet, and dogs usually cock a leg to urinate when they mature, so you'll have most success with a small-breed bitch.

How do I house-train my puppy?

First learn to recognize when the puppy needs to toilet (see page 64). Take him to the designated area at the required time. Leave the pup's last dropping in this area to indicate that this is the right place to go. Take him there when he

Stroke rather than pat your puppy to reward him. Try both actions on yourself and you'll see that the former is far more comfortable and soothing than the latter.

Don't unconsciously reward your dog's inappropriate behaviour, otherwise your puppy will assume that such actions are acceptable. For example, do not allow your puppy to go through a doorway before you (which is a reward in itself, as he has done what he wanted, when he wanted); make him wait while you pass through, then allow him to follow and reward with praise and/or a treat.

How should I admonish my puppy when necessary – do I smack him?

Smacking your puppy will make him frightened and less responsive. It can also sow the seeds of aggression towards humans. It's better to manipulate situations so that your puppy does the right thing and can be rewarded for it.

Whenever your puppy spontaneously offers behaviours you want, use the opportunity to further his training. If he lies down beside you without pestering you for attention, reward him. He will learn which behaviours and actions make for a pleasant life, and will strive always to perform that code of behaviour.

ABOVE LEFT Ignore the puppy when he pesters you for attention and he will learn that his unwanted actions are unrewarding.

LEFT When your puppy is displaying the behaviour you want, praise him for it.

Should I allow my puppy to bite at my hands and shoelaces while playing?

No. If encouraged or unchecked, play-biting tends to become increasingly severe. Eventually the dog is of an age where he really hurts, or causes an accident, and frightens his human targets. Such a habit is difficult to cure once ingrained.

Rather than your hand, give your pup toys to chew and play with. Never tap him on the nose as this encourages biting. 'Yelp' loudly when he bites, move away from and ignore him; only reward him with attention when he refrains from biting.

A nasty-tasting anti-bite liquid (available from pet stores) sprayed on your hands and shoelaces can be an effective deterrent – just one taste and your puppy won't be keen to repeat the unpleasant experience!

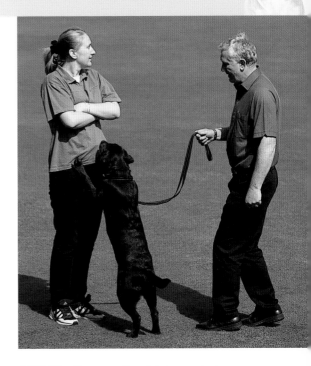

ABOVE When the puppy attempts to jump up, turn your head to avoid eye contact with him, fold your arms out of the way and ignore him.

How can I stop my puppy jumping up at people?

Don't encourage him to do so, and politely ask other people to discourage it too. It is unfair to let your pet jump up at you as a puppy and then scold him for doing so as an adult.

Acknowledge him only when he stays down and settles, which he will when he realizes that jumping up provokes no reaction from you. This way he'll learn that the action gains no reward, while keeping all four paws on the ground results in a more pleasant experience.

How can I stop visitors encouraging my puppy to play roughly?

It is only good manners that people invited into your house should follow your rules. This applies as much to giving your puppy attention as to anything else. Advise your visitors how to behave around your pet and make it clear that rough play is banned, explaining why.

If, despite your request, you still feel visitors' behaviour towards your pet is inappropriate, then for safety's sake remove the puppy from the room. Put him in another room, or in the garden, with an activity toy or stuffed Kong (see page 48) to keep him happily occupied.

How do I stop my 20-week-old puppy threatening to bite if anyone goes near his food?

Food is important to dogs and they can become possessive about it. You must teach your pup that a human near his food bowl represents no threat to his meal, and assert yourself as pack leader so that the pup eats only how and when you dictate. Here's how to do this:

1 Put the puppy on a leash and put down his food bowl.

2 Use the leash to prevent him from eating and say 'leave'.

3 Wait until he looks at you for permission to eat, then say 'eat' and allow him to do so. Praise him for his patience.

4 As he eats, add treats to the bowl so that he views people and hands near his bowl as non-threatening.

5 If he growls or threatens to bite, pull him away from the bowl and repeat steps 2–4. He will soon learn that being threatening isn't rewarding and will stop the behaviour.

ABOVE Leftover fruit and veg are suitable scraps for a puppy, as are boneless fish and meat. Don't feed him from the table though!

he's not getting enough food. Bear in mind, though, that puppies are naturally greedy and will eat until exhausted if given the chance.

Fast eaters rarely suffer problems, so this is nothing to be alarmed about unless a digestive upset or discomfort is apparent. Placing large, heavy, rubber balls (Kong type, see page 48) in the food will help slow down eating if necessary.

My puppy gobbles his food. Should we give him more to eat, and will eating so fast make him ill?

Make sure you are providing the recommended amount of suitable food per meal (see page 49). Also check that your puppy is the correct weight for his age and size. It is possible that he's not getting enough nutrition for his body's needs, either because he has worms or

Can we give our puppy leftovers from our meals?

Most leftovers are fine for dogs but avoid sugary and spicy foods, and small bones. Treat leftovers as part of the daily food amount, otherwise your puppy may put on more weight than is good for him. Vegetables and fruit (cooked and fresh), cereals, gravy, boneless fish and meat scraps are most suitable, as these mimic the dog's natural diet.

Why does our puppy chew things he shouldn't?

Puppies' milk teeth start to be replaced by their permanent teeth between the ages of 3 and 6 months. During this time he is likely to chew anything he can get his teeth on, in order to alleviate itching and discomfort in his gums and to help the permanent teeth erupt.

Be tidy and put things you don't want your puppy to chew – especially electric cables – out of reach wherever possible, and keep him out of areas in the house you particularly don't want redesigned!

BELOW Bear in mind that puppies do not differentiate between things you don't mind them chewing and those you do.

How can we stop our puppy chewing inappropriate items?

Never encourage your puppy to pull or chew at clothing during play sessions. Don't give him discarded items of clothing or footwear to play with, and don't allow him to chew sticks or lumps of wood, since table legs may well be his next 'victim'.

A bored puppy will find entertainment, so provide him with chew toys to gnaw on; a big boiled marrow bone will also be much appreciated (see page 50). If he has his own things to chew, he's less likely to destroy yours.

Spray items that your puppy persists in chewing with an anti-bite liquid (available from pet stores) – the bitter taste is usually enough to cure the habit.

WHEN IS A PUPPY CONSIDERED AN ADULT DOG?

Puppies usually reach sexual maturity at 6 months of age. Mental/physical maturity follows at around 18 months, depending on the size and breed.

NEWBORN Dependent on his mother for food, care, help in defecating and urinating, and protection.

2–3 WEEKS Senses of sight, smell and hearing begin to operate. Teeth begin to appear and he learns to walk and lap formula milk foods. Ability to urinate and defecate unaided develops. Humans can begin to handle him to start the socialization process.

4–5 WEEKS Able to stand better and toddle around on increasingly steady legs. Eating more solid puppy food. Starts to play with siblings, wag tail and yap. Leaves the sleeping area to toilet.

6 WEEKS Full use of ears, eyes and facial/ear expressions more evident. Weaning proper starts as he's no longer totally dependent on his mother's milk. First vaccinations can be done.

7–19 WEEKS Second vaccinations can be done at 10 weeks. When fully weaned is independent of his mother, and if socialized with humans and other animals, he's ready to go to a new home.

3–6 MONTHS (JUVENILE) Chewing and mouthing are common during teething. Regular training helps him learn his place within the family, along with obedience and manners. Concentration and ability to learn increase with age.

6–18 MONTHS (ADOLESCENT) The 'teenage' phase, when he's likely to become unruly and try to assert dominance if unchecked and handled inappropriately. Sexual maturity is reached. The most difficult time for owners!

18 MONTHS AND OVER (ADULT) Character is fully formed, though refinements will still occur until he settles down at around 3 years of age.

Is it a good idea to have our puppy neutered?

Yes, for two main reasons. The first is to prevent unwanted pregnancies in females, the second to help prevent both sexes wandering off in search of mates.

A bitch is in season (receptive to mating) twice a year in most cases and can have up to eight or more pups per litter. With unplanned pregnancies presenting so many pups to find homes for it's small wonder that rescue centres are full to capacity. Few inmates are lucky enough to find homes and the destruction figure worldwide is simply staggering.

BELOW **Before and after neutering; male anatomy in top pictures, female in bottom two.**

Having escaped to find mates, dogs put themselves at risk of getting lost, catching or passing on disease, or being involved in an accident – many road accidents per year are attributed to wandering dogs. For further information on neutering, see below and opposite.

At what age should we have our puppy neutered to prevent him breeding?

This can be done when he or she reaches sexual maturity at around 6 months old, or at any time afterwards. Some vets prefer to wait until a bitch has had her first season and then neuter (spay) at 9 months, while others will not spay if

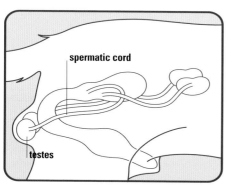

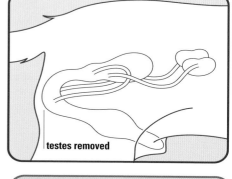

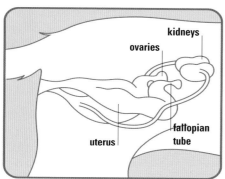

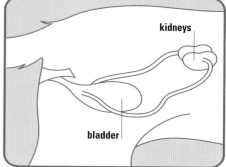

the bitch is in season, preferring to wait until 3 months have elapsed afterwards to allow the blood flow through the reproductive organs to return to normal. Neutering in dogs is called castration.

Is the neutering procedure always safe?

As with any operation involving anaesthetic, there is always a risk. But modern veterinary procedures and safer anaesthetics ensure this is minimal.

Dogs that have heart, circulatory, respiration or other debilitating ailments (which may not be apparent prior to the operation) are at particular risk from the effects of the anaesthetic and surgery. If you wish, you can request that your vet gives your puppy a thorough check-up before neutering to ascertain that it is safe to carry out the procedure.

Will neutering have any detrimental long-term effects on our puppy?

It is extremely rare for dogs to suffer detrimental affects to their health following neutering. Occasionally, failure to heal properly after surgery due to infection setting in can prove a problem, as can subsequent incontinence in bitches (see page 183), although these instances are few and far between.

The advantages of having your pet neutered outweigh any possible disadvantages, so many pet owners feel the risk is worth taking.

What happens when neutering is carried out?

The procedure for spaying females is more involved than the castration of males. This means that neutering takes longer in bitches and is more expensive.

Spaying
The ovaries, Fallopian tubes and uterus (womb) are removed under a general anaesthetic (see illustration opposite). An incision is made from the navel towards the hindlegs, through which the organs are removed. The wound is closed via stitches that are removed 10–14 days later, unless soluble stitches (which gradually dissolve) are used.

Castration
The testicles (testes) and a small section of the spermatic cords are removed through a small incision in the scrotum. The incision is then stitched as for bitches.

My 5-month-old puppy lost a tooth while chewing a toy. Will it grow back?

Puppies shed their baby teeth between the ages of 3 and 6 months. It is likely that your puppy lost a milk (non-permanent) tooth, which is normal. If you look, you will probably see the replacement permanent tooth crowning (coming through the gum). The first two permanent teeth to crown are the two centre teeth (incisors) on the top jaw, and the last are the large corner (canine) teeth in both top and bottom jaws.

How many teeth does an adult dog have?

An adult dog has 42 permanent teeth. They comprise:
- Eight premolars in the upper jaw (four either side) and six in the lower (three per side).
- Six molars in the upper jaw (three per side) and six in the lower (three per side).
- Six incisors in the upper jaw (three per side) and six in the lower (three per side).
- Two canine teeth in both the upper and lower jaws – one at each of the front corners.

Sometimes the milk teeth are not shed before the permanent teeth come through (particularly in Toy breeds) and this can cause discomfort as well as distorting the shape of the mouth. Eating and digestion problems can result. In these cases, veterinary attention should be sought.

ABOVE **Most dogs don't need their teeth brushed, although a soft diet may make it necessary.**

Should I clean my puppy's teeth and will this stop his breath smelling?

Look at your puppy's diet first. Fed a diet comprising plenty of solid, crunchy or tough food to chew on, which stimulates his gum circulation and removes the accumulated plaque, your puppy's teeth should not need cleaning, and his breath will be as sweet as can be expected.

Convenience dog foods tend to be soft and cling to the teeth with no means of removing the resulting sludge, which eventually turns into hard tartar. If your young dog receives such a diet, then clean his teeth weekly with a special canine toothbrush and paste (available from pet stores or your vet) to maintain oral health.

Our puppy is very boisterous – is this normal?

Like young children, puppies are enormously energetic and curious. Play and investigation is high on the list of priorities, so you can expect them to be lively when awake. It would be unusual if your puppy were not and you should suspect something is wrong with him.

It is important not to let natural energy get out of hand. If the puppy gets overexcited and rough, remove him from the room or place him in his crate (sanctuary) to 'cool down'. Don't admonish him – simply wait until he settles before allowing him to rejoin you.

Our puppy seems scared of other dogs. Why is this and how can we teach him to be less afraid?

It's likely that your puppy has not been adequately socialized with other dogs. Alternatively, he may have had a bad experience with another dog.

The best way of overcoming this problem is to take him along to puppy socialization classes at least once a week. This will help him to integrate with other young dogs around the same age as him, and learn the intricacies of pack code in a safe environment. As he grows older you can progress to training classes, again on a regular basis, to help you learn how to train him and for him to learn how to interact sociably with other dogs.

How old should my puppy be before I start agility training with him?

Don't ask your puppy to do anything too strenuous, such as jumping, until he's physically mature. If you do, you'll risk damaging his developing bones, joints, tendons and ligaments.

However, you can 'play' at teaching him to weave in and out of obstacles, go through tunnels, and walk over poles and tyres on the ground, as he will find these activities enjoyable if you treat it all as a game.

Consult a vet who specializes in canines as to when your puppy will be physically mature enough for strenuous activities, as this varies between breeds.

How do I train my 7-month-old pup? He seems to ignore everything I tell him.

If the puppy is ignoring your bidding, then you are not directing him properly. From the age of 6 months, a 'teenage' dog is likely to 'try it on', and how you handle him at this stage is crucial. Get it wrong and you'll have persistent problems that you'll struggle to solve without expert advice.

You'll find that it pays dividends to enrol in a puppy socialization/training class, as attending on a regular basis will teach you how to communicate with your pet and what methods you should employ in order to get him to behave as you require.

ABOVE Their natural curiosity means that puppies enjoy discovering and doing new things, but take care not to overtax their immature bodies.

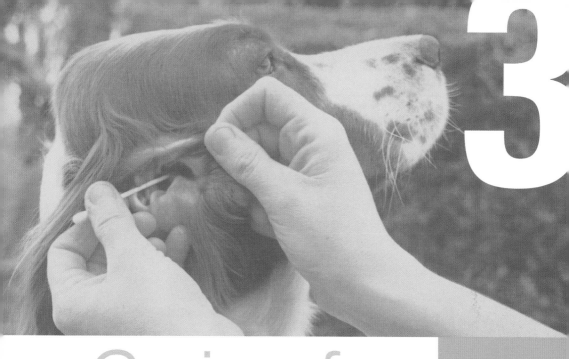

Caring for your dog

Do you need a licence to own a dog?

Dog licences are required by law in some countries, but not others. Check with your local authority to discover whether or not you need a licence for your pet.

All dog owners should, however, ensure that their pet wears an identity tag (in some countries it is a legal requirement), so that in the event of him getting lost or being involved in an accident he can be identified (see pages 35–36).

How much does it cost to keep a dog?

When calculating the cost of keeping your pet, you need to look at several areas. The first is the initial expense of buying your dog and the basic equipment with which to look after him. Then comes the cost of neutering and identification marking. Finally, there are the routine annual expenses:

- Food
- Internal and external parasite treatments
- Professional grooming charges (where applicable)
- Annual vet checks and vaccination booster
- Trips to the vet in the event of injury/illness
- Replacement grooming equipment and food/water bowls

- Treats
- Replacement toys
- Training fees
- Insurance premium
- Boarding kennel charges when you are on holiday
- Household repairs, if your dog turns out to be a demolition expert!

If a dog could choose his owner, what qualities would he be looking for?

Dogs respond best to calm, consistent handling. An ideal owner would be someone who can devote enough time to fulfilling a dog's needs for care and attention, and who is patient, kind, fair, understanding, self-controlled, reliable, and firm enough to implement house/training rules and stick to them.

Know your own limits: if you don't like hairy, slobbery dogs, for example, then don't be swayed into getting one. If you do, both you and your pet are likely to end up being miserable in each other's company.

RIGHT Learn to understand your dog in order to create a mutually rewarding relationship with him.

Do you have to have a big house and garden to own a dog?

Ideally, your house should be large enough to accommodate your family and your chosen type of dog with plenty of space for everyone. If you don't have a suitable-sized garden in which to exercise him, then you must be prepared to take your dog for two or three walks daily, with somewhere to let him loose off-leash for a good run.

Big, energetic working dogs do not thrive in small, cramped living spaces with minimal room outside to release pent-up energy. For example, a small flat is no place to keep a German Shepherd Dog or English Mastiff, and doing so is usually a recipe for disaster.

What equipment do I need before I get a dog?

Basic equipment is the same as for a puppy (see page 46). In summary, you will need:
- Collar, identity tag and three-in-one training leash
- Food and water bowls
- Bed large enough for the dog to stretch out in to rest and sleep, plus bedding
- Old towels or soft rags (to dry off wet, muddy dogs)
- First-aid kit
- Grooming tools
- Toys
- Dog food
- Training crate/travel pen.

A poop scoop is a must-have for walks and clearing the toileting area in the garden. Buy a purpose-made scoop and biodegradable bags from a pet store, or improvise with nappy (diaper) bags – simply put your hand inside the bag, scoop the poop, turn the bag inside out and dispose of it appropriately, either at home or in bins designed for the purpose.

What's the best type of collar and leash for my dog?

Collars come in many designs, and selecting one can be confusing. The most suitable types are a broad leather or fabric collar, or a half-check (check-choke),

BELOW Half-check collars and three-in-one training leashes are the usual choice of dog trainers.

which is three-quarters fabric or leather and one-quarter chain link. All these styles are kinder and more comfortable than narrow or metal collars. Avoid using check (choke) chain collars, which consist solely of chain links and tighten like a slip knot when pulled, as these can hurt your dog.

For a lead, the three-in-one training leash is most practical (see page 46). You can use it as a short, medium or long leash. Choose one that is appropriate for the size of your dog, and which fits your own hand comfortably.

What is the best type of bed and bedding for a dog?

Moulded plastic beds are best because they are tough, light and easy to clean. Higher on three sides, they help prevent draughts affecting your dog, too. Wicker and fabric beds may look prettier, but they do not stand the test of time and soon appear grubby and worn.

ABOVE **The only drawback to veterinary fleece bedding is that it is quite expensive.**

Veterinary fleece bedding is the best choice for bedding as it's light to handle, warm in cold weather but not too warm in hot weather, lasts well, is easy to wash and dries quickly. Alternatively, you can use old blankets or duvets.

I'm thinking of getting a dog as a present for someone. Is this a good idea?

Buying a dog as a gift for someone is not to be recommended. Can you guarantee that the recipient is willing to take on the responsibility of owning a dog, and has the time and money to care for it?

Sadly, too many dogs bought as gifts end up in rescue centres once their novelty value has waned. There is a commendable saying: 'A dog is for life, not just for Christmas', but still rescue centres are full to overflowing. Many reputable breeders will not sell their puppies at Christmas, or for presents if they are informed that the dog is to be 'gift-wrapped'.

Is there anything vital I should be aware of before offering a rescue dog a home?

If the dog was brought up badly, then it may well have behaviour problems. It may be aggressive, destructive, disobedient or unclean in the house – or possibly all four.

It is possible to rehabilitate a 'lost cause', which will be rewarding, but this takes time and patience. Consider whether you have the desire to tackle

ABOVE Dogs in rescue centres are there for a reason. In all cases it is through no fault of their own, but due to their owners being no longer able to care for them, for a variety of reasons.

ABOVE RIGHT Many rescue dogs make fantastic family pets. However, be aware that it can take a while for them to settle in to new homes. Some may not tolerate children or other animals.

such a challenge, and are willing to enlist professional training help to overcome the inevitable difficulties you will face.

Why do some rescue centres want to meet the whole family when you choose a dog?

This allows the staff to assess all the family members, in order to make the best possible match. They also want to see how the dog reacts to his potential owners. The staff do not want to hand over a dog to what might prove to be an unsuitable home. Although it may be a nuisance arranging a suitable time when all can attend the rescue centre, it is done in your and the dog's best interests.

Do I need to insure my dog?

It makes sense to insure your pet. Veterinary costs can be high should your dog require medical attention – operations or a prolonged course of treatment are particularly expensive – while a lawsuit for personal or property damage caused by your dog could prove ruinous.

Ideally, pet insurance should be considered a necessity rather than a luxury, but do shop around for the best (not necessarily the cheapest) deal and read the small print before parting with your money. Some insurance companies insist dogs are vaccinated before issuing policies, or refuse a claim if vaccinations are not kept up to date.

How should I go about grooming my dog?

Your approach to grooming will depend on your dog's coat type. There is advice on the equipment you'll need on page 47 and on how often to groom on page 30.

Depending on your dog's size, it's often easier to groom him on a table. Place a rubber mat on it to give him a firm footing. It is useful to have someone to help you until he gets used to this and stays put. Never leave your pet unattended on the table, in case he jumps off and hurts himself.

Make grooming a pleasant experience so that your dog learns to enjoy it. Getting impatient will simply cause both you and your dog a great deal of stress and nothing good will be achieved. If he becomes restless, finish on a good note and try again later.

You can buy books and videos that demonstrate the best way to groom different breeds of dog – look out for them in pet stores and advertisements in dog magazines.

And how about bathing him?

An adult dog will need to be bathed from time to time. Advice on bathing is also provided on pages 52–53. Never bath a dog with a matted coat as this will only make the tangles worse. Groom out the coat first, gently teasing out all the knots right down to the roots. If your dog's coat is very matted, then it is often kinder to have it professionally clipped off rather than struggling with it.

What routine care does a dog need?

To maintain your pet's mental and physical health, certain routine procedures should be carried out on a daily, monthly and yearly basis. These are listed in the table below.

ROUTINE CARE

Daily

Exercise.

Feed; clean food bowl.

Refresh water bowl after cleaning it.

Monitor behaviour.

Groom.

Check eliminations for abnormalities.

Check collar fit for comfort.

Continue ongoing training, perhaps at a weekly/fortnightly training class.

Monthly

Check weight.

Check for fleas.

De-worm every 3 months.

Six-monthly vet check for elderly dogs.

Yearly

Vaccination boosters.

Vet check.

How can I make my house and garden safe for a dog?

There are a number of areas to consider. First, make your garden escape-proof (see page 52). Then follow the guidelines below.

- Keep harmful products such as garden chemicals, detergents, motor oils, medicines and so on out of your pet's reach.
- Lock away sharp implements when you are not using them.
- Don't put down vermin poisons.
- Keep your pet inside when mowing the lawn or trimming hedges.
- Keep your pet out of the bathroom when running a bath (for human/pet safety, always run the cold water first and then add hot).
- Wherever possible, contain electric cables within conduit.

- Don't leave sewing equipment such as needles and pins lying around.
- Don't subject your dog to loud TV or stereo noise that could damage his sensitive hearing.

I have heard that dogs need their own 'personal space'. How do I provide this?

'Personal space' is an area the dog can escape to when he needs to rest or sleep undisturbed. He may also retire to it for security if he senses that you are not in the best of moods, until he feels it is safe to venture out.

BELOW **Make sure your garden is escape-proof. Inspect your boundary daily before you let your dog out and repair gaps or holes immediately.**

It is essential for your pet's mental wellbeing that he has this special area, which can be his bed or crate – position it in a quiet area of the house. It is important that family members don't bother the dog in his sanctuary.

ABOVE Just as we like to have time by ourselves sometimes to recharge our batteries, so too do dogs.

How can I ensure my children and dog get on well together?

Children must be taught to respect the dog and learn how to handle and speak to him correctly. Dogs can be very tolerant with babies and young children, but this is not something you should put to the test.

Teach children not to grab at the dog, and insist that they leave him alone when he is eating and resting. Make sure your children teach your dog only good behaviour and play only acceptable games with him. Show them how and where he likes to be petted gently.

Never leave your children alone with your dog, no matter how placid he normally is, as unsupervised children are apt to tease pets unmercifully.

How much daily exercise does a dog need?

This depends on the type, size, breed, health and age of the dog. Some breeds require more physical activity than

ABOVE Avoid walking your dog in the heat of the day, and take water and a fold-up bowl with you on long hikes if you are unsure whether the route offers a clean water supply.

others in order to remain happy and healthy, although some that you might imagine need lots of exercise, such as Greyhounds, in fact do not. Young and old dogs should be exercised carefully within their physical limits to avoid causing stress to either growing or ageing bones, muscles and other tissues.

How much daily exercise a dog needs also depends on his fitness and weight; dogs, just like people, can become overweight and unfit; they need to get fit gradually in order to avoid overtaxing 'soft' bodies.

Do I need to buy a dog coat for my pet when the weather is cold and wet?

Thin- or short-coated and older dogs will appreciate the protection a coat offers, to keep them dry and warm. Slender, fine-coated breeds, such as Whippets, have little in the way of a coat and body fat to insulate them against wet and cold, while older dogs' bodies are not as efficient at generating and maintaining heat as their younger counterparts.

You may also find putting a coat on your dog useful during wet weather to reduce the cleaning and drying time needed after a walk. 'Boots' are available to keep paws clean and dry too.

How can I keep my car seats clean, dry and odour-free when taking my dog for a walk?

The best way to avoid the inside of your car resembling a kennel is to buy waterproof seat covers and a boot (trunk) liner. Although better-quality ones are quite expensive, they will soon prove a sound investment as not only do they fit the seats better, they also last and wash well, retaining their shape. Furniture covers are also a wise buy if you are at all house-proud.

Ask the instructor and other owners at your local dog training club if they can recommend particular makes or brands of furniture and car seat covers on a tried-and-tested basis. You will find seat covers advertised in dog magazines and on sale in pet stores.

What's the best way to dispose of dog faeces?

There are several ways to deal with faeces deposited in your garden or out on a walk. Find out if there are local authority bins specially provided for the disposal of dog faeces nearby. If not, wrap the faeces well in newspaper or a biodegradable bag and put them in your household rubbish (check with your local authority first). Alternatively, you can buy a 'dog loo' that you install in the garden, although reports on their effectiveness are mixed.

Consult your vet practice or local waste disposal company regarding the disposal of waste from a dog receiving radiation treatment.

ABOVE It is important to dispose of dog faeces carefully when your dog eliminates, to help reduce the risk of disease spread (via worms and viruses) and to keep areas clean – no one likes stepping in dog mess!

What's the most suitable food for a dog?

Dogs are not generally fussy eaters. They thrive on a diet that is not dissimilar to that of humans, albeit with more protein, comprising foods of animal origin, cereals, root vegetables and fats. The most suitable diet for a dog is one that contains:

- Protein, carbohydrates and fats.
- Vitamins – A, B-group, D and E; vitamin C is produced in the body.
- Minerals – the most important being calcium, phosphorus and sodium chloride. These and other essential minerals, such as copper and zinc, occur naturally in meat, cereals and other food ingredients.
- Fibre and water in balanced proportions.

I want to give my dog a totally natural home-made diet. Is this a good idea?

It can be difficult to ensure that a home-made diet provides all the essential nutrients your pet needs to promote and maintain his health. There are commercially produced dog foods that state they do not contain artificial additives but are balanced nutritionally, so it may be worth your while checking up on these as they are easier to feed than preparing fresh foods from scratch.

If you are determined to feed only natural products to your pet, then it would be wise to read up on the subject – there are several excellent books

ABOVE Commercially produced dog foods are nutritionally balanced and are available in (left to right) wet, semi-moist and dry varieties.

RIGHT Many people feel that a natural diet promotes better health than convenience dog foods that contain genetically modified organisms, artificial preservatives and colours, and so on.

available, written by canine nutrition experts, on feeding home-made diets to both adult dogs and puppies.

How much food does a dog need? Should this be fed all in one meal, and at a certain time of day?

The table on page 88 provides an approximate guide to food quantities. Decrease or increase the amounts as necessary, depending on your pet's condition.

It is preferable to split the daily amount into two or three portions and feed these meals at different times of the day. This is especially important in the case of big, deep-chested dogs, such as Great Danes and German Shepherds, so that the stomach isn't overloaded, thus helping to avoid gastric ailments. Additionally, more than one meal a day provides interaction and interest.

It is better not to feed at the same time each day, otherwise you dog learns to expect this and will be upset if his meal fails to materialize at the expected time – for example, if you are late home from work. He may then turn to inappropriate behaviour, such as chewing furniture, to vent his frustration. Varying feeding times will also help to keep your pet's food motivation high, which helps with subsequent training.

WET FOOD QUANTITIES BY WEIGHT

IDEAL WEIGHT OF ADULT DOG	APPROXIMATE DAILY FOOD REQUIREMENT
2 kg (5 lb)	110–140 g (4–5 oz)
5 kg (10 lb)	200–280 g (7–10 oz)
10 kg (25 lb)	400–570 g (14 oz–1 lb 4 oz)
20 kg (50 lb)	680–900 g (1 lb 8 oz–2 lb)
35 kg (75 lb)	900g–1.1 kg (2 lb–2 lb 8 oz)
45 kg (100 lb)	1.25–1.6 kg (2 lb 12 oz–3 lb 8 oz)
70 kg (150 lb)	1.7–2.5 kg (3 lb 12 oz–5 lb 8 oz)

How often should I clean my dog's water and food bowls, and with what?

Wash your dog's bowls daily. Bowls quickly become soiled with saliva and old food, both of which harbour germs and soon start to smell. A solution of common salt and hot water (2 tablespoons to 1 litre/2 pints) does the job admirably, but ensure that you rinse them well with cold water afterwards to remove salt residue.

You can also buy dog-bowl cleaning fluids that are non-toxic and non-scented. Again, make sure the bowls are rinsed well after cleaning.

Does my dog need extra vitamins and minerals added to his food?

If you are feeding a good-quality dog food, then your pet should not need extra vitamins and minerals. A deficiency in essential nutrients will usually show up in your pet's general appearance, health and demeanour – symptoms include a dull coat, lack of energy, allergies and digestive upsets. If you notice such symptoms, try changing his food brand for a better-quality one and see if it makes any difference (allow a couple of weeks for any improvement to become apparent).

Dogs fed on a home-made diet may also benefit from food supplementation – ask your vet for advice if you feel your dog is lacking 'something' in his diet.

My dog will now only eat cooked chicken. How can I tempt him back onto his usual dog food?

Stop feeding him the chicken and offer only his usual food, or try changing the brand. Do not give him any food treats, snacks or your leftovers in between his

ABOVE Remove uneaten food after 20 minutes (and if semi-moist/wet, dispose of it), so that your dog learns to eat up when meals are offered.

meals. Dogs won't starve themselves for days on end unless there is a good physical reason (it's worth getting your vet to check your pet over to eliminate this), or the food is 'off', so selective fussy feeders are usually cured after a day or two of being offered nothing but their regular diet at set times.

How will I know if I'm giving my dog too much or too little food?

The quantity of food a dog needs daily to provide for his body's demands depends on several factors. These include his size, activity level, age, individual nature and the temperature of his surroundings. For an approximate guide to daily food requirements, see the chart opposite on page 88.

ABOVE **Most dogs are naturally greedy and will eat as much food as is put in front of them, so it's tempting to overfeed them thinking they must still be hungry. However, it's important to feed to maintain correct body condition, otherwise your dog will become obese.**

Young dogs and those in work, or which are very active on a daily basis, need more food (calories) per day than the average pet dog, whereas an old, inactive dog will require fewer calories. Give too much food and your dog will get fat, give too little and he'll become thin. Ask your vet what the ideal weight is for your dog, and aim to keep him at this.

Could my dog's recurrent flaky skin problem be diet-related?

Yes, it certainly could be. First, have your dog checked by a vet to eliminate the possibility of skin infections through parasites or other ailments; then try changing your pet's diet to see if this makes any difference. Just as humans can have allergies to certain food ingredients, so too can dogs.

Choose a hypo-allergenic brand of complete food and treats (if fed) – these will have no added artificial colours, flavours, antioxidants or preservatives – and allow about 6 weeks to see if your dog's skin improves. If not, try another brand: it's a matter of trial and error, so don't expect a quick fix.

Many dogs with skin complaints have been found to thrive on a rice and lamb, white meat or fish-based diet, as they are allergic to wheat and beef.

Is it all right to give my dog the leftover bones from roasted meat joints?

Never give your dog small roasted bones (especially poultry bones). These tend to splinter when chewed, presenting a real risk of digestive tract injuries. Large bones are fairly safe when given to small dogs with small, weak jaws, but never give them to powerfully jawed pets to avoid the potential of harm.

My dog loves eating our leftover food – is this all right?

Generally speaking, table scraps are fine in moderate amounts. Do not overfeed, as leftovers can be too rich for dogs, and avoid spicy foods and those which contain alcohol or chocolate. Treat scraps as part of your dog's daily food allowance and not an addition to it, otherwise he will become obese.

Some dogs do seem to enjoy eating the remains of a curry, but bear in mind that many are terrible scavengers and will eat any table scraps put in front of them, despite the potential for an unpleasant digestive disturbance later. It's safer to put leftover curry in the bin rather than feed it to your dog.

How can I minimize the mess my dog makes when eating?

Make sure his bowl is large enough to contain the food adequately. The bigger the bowl, the less mess you'll get – usually.

However, some dogs insist on picking the food out of their bowl and dropping it on the floor. If the above advice doesn't work, and placing the bowl on a large feeding mat is not an acceptable solution, then feed your dog outside where at least the mess he makes won't spoil the kitchen floor surface.

Is there a way of preventing my Spaniel's ears dangling in his food?

Some owners of long-eared dogs employ a simple solution to this problem. They use hair (pony tail) bands or clothes pegs to secure the ears on top of their pet's head while he is eating, which prevents them from dangling in the food. This is very effective – just make sure that the pegs or bands are not too tight, otherwise they will case discomfort.

Hair clips are sometimes suggested, but these are too tight unless just long hair on the dog's ears is clipped together.

TOP Do not allow your children to feed the dog from the table. Bad habits will result.

ABOVE Special 'Spaniel' bowls stand high off the floor and help prevent food-covered ears; they are also useful aids for dogs with back problems. These bowls are available from pet stores or by mail-order from pet product companies.

Should I change my dog's regular diet to give him some variety?

Dog foods come in all manner of flavours and textures, even 'gourmet' varieties. However, this is mainly to appeal to owners rather than their pets. Unlike us, dogs do not get bored with eating the same thing on a daily basis, so it is not necessary to change your pet's diet unless he fails to thrive on it. Changing the variety often can produce a fussy eater, so while he's eating up and seems fit and healthy it's safer to continue feeding the same food.

Where is the best place to store an opened can of dog food?

The fridge is the best place to store canned dog meat once it has been opened. You can leave it in the can – for hygiene, either cover with cling film (plastic wrap) or use a plastic lid designed for dog meat cans which you can buy from pet stores – or decant it into another container if you wish, but it should be used up within 2 days.

What's the best type of diet to feed a dog who is prone to tummy upsets?

A vet check will determine whether the tummy upsets are due to an ailment or to worm infestation. If the diagnosis is simply that your pet has a 'delicate tummy', then it's a case of eliminating by trial and error the foods and treats (if

given) that cause him problems. Start with red meat and wheat-based and dairy foods, as well as those with artificial ingredients. Avoid giving him table scraps; if these are too rich, the result may be vomiting and diarrhoea.

A hypo-allergenic brand of complete dog food often proves helpful in such cases. If not, then it's worth trying a natural home-made diet (see page 86). Consulting a holistic vet regarding a suitable diet would probably prove helpful.

My dog loves raw vegetables as well as fruit. Will this harm him?

Raw vegetables and fruit are rich in natural antioxidants (which are beneficial to health), minerals and vitamins. Many dogs love carrots, green

BELOW **Fresh fruit and vegetables can add variety to your dog's diet.**

leafy vegetables and apples, so a daily helping of what he fancies in this respect won't do your dog any harm. However, anything eaten in excess can be harmful, so bear this in mind.

Avoid feeding decaying fruit and vegetables, and green (unripe) potato peelings. Onions and garlic can have detrimental effects on some dogs if eaten in quantity (relative to the size of the dog), so exercise caution when giving these vegetables mixed with other foods.

What are the most suitable toys for a dog?

The same safety principles that apply to toys suitable for puppies are also relevant to adult dogs (see pages 47–48). As well as being play items, toys are invaluable bonding and training aids. Choose a selection of toys that will represent the different values shown in the table below.

Keep the low-value toys for all-time access, and the medium-value ones for shared play sessions and training to reward and reinforce desirable behaviour. The high-value toys ('supertoys') should be kept as an ultimate enticement or reward for special achievement.

Are there any indestructible toys?

Some dogs are extremely rough with their toys and destroy them almost straight away, which can be expensive. If this is a problem, avoid soft toys and those made of thin plastic that your dog can easily rip and chew bits off. Choose more robust items, like heavy plain rubber toys (such as those in the Kong range, see page 48) or tough flavoured synthetic or plastic chew toys (such as those in the Nylabone range, see page 48). Be vigilant when your dog is playing with a toy. It is easy for a dog to choke or

TOY VALUES

Low value	Medium value	High value
Rubber rings	Tug toys	Squeaky toys
Home-made play items, such as cardboard tubes from toilet and kitchen rolls	Raggers (fabric toys designed to be grabbed and shaken by the dog)	Frisbees
	Flavoured chew toys	Activity toys (in which treats are placed)
	Balls and other chase toys such as balls on ropes	

ABOVE AND RIGHT Heavy rope raggers and Kong toys are extremely durable.

injure himself on chewed-off bits of hard plastic. Some dogs gain a good deal of satisfaction from shredding toys, in which case you can provide yours with an old leather football or home-made item to destroy to fulfil this desire.

Why should you not let a dog play with sticks?

Sticks can break and splinter when chewed, often resulting in mouth injuries. If swallowed, they can cause digestive tract injuries. A stick can also impale a dog if he trips over while carrying it, causing serious injury or even death.

Is it all right for my dog to play with stones?

Although many dogs like to play with and chase after stones, it isn't safe for them to do so. As well as the dangers associated with choking on or swallowing them, chewing stones can often result in prematurely worn and broken teeth. It's far better to encourage your dog to play with more appropriate items (see pictures above).

What are the most suitable games to play with a dog?

Avoid rough games, instead encouraging calm, responsive play. Use toys to gain your pet's attention, elicit the desired responses and then reward him for them.

Dogs love to chase balls and other items thrown for them. Encourage your dog not only to go after them (which you can turn into a 'send away'), but also to pick them up and bring them back to you ('carry' and 'retrieve') – see page 50. Teach him to surrender toys without making a fuss.

Hiding toys or treats around the house or garden can become an entertaining game of hide-and-seek for both parties, while stashing them in a cardboard box full of scrunched-up newspaper becomes an enjoyable 'hunt and find' game.

I enjoy play-wrestling with my dog, but lately he's become too rough. How can I stop this?

'Tug of war' and 'wrestling' are unsuitable 'games' to play with dogs. While such activities can be great fun initially, they can become unpleasant if the dog gets overexcited and aims to dominate and win the 'match'.

You must stop encouraging 'play-wrestling', and ignore the dog if he tries to engage you in it. Wait until he's calm, then play a more suitable game with him (see page 94). When he realizes that 'good games' are more rewarding than 'bad games', he will refrain from the latter.

BOTTOM Although generally thought of as a traditional play item for dogs, sticks can, in fact, prove lethal to them.

BELOW Don't allow rough behaviour in a puppy as it can become a real problem in an adult dog.

How can I make my dog more affectionate and playful?

Like some humans, some dogs are naturally more aloof than others. If this is the case, then you'll have to respect his need 'to be alone' and find other aspects about him to enjoy, such as walks, grooming and his comforting presence.

You could try different tactics with him, such as inventing interesting games involving unusual toys and smelly treats that he finds too tempting to ignore; perhaps even try agility classes.

Perhaps your approaches to him are too boisterous or loud and are putting him off, especially if he has a sensitive nature. Review how you handle your dog and try a different approach, but don't expect him to respond overnight.

What is the correct way to pick up a dog?

To pick up and carry a dog comfortably for both parties, follow the steps below:

1 Crouch down and gently but firmly gather your dog to you, with one arm around his chest to keep him from breaking free and the other arm under his bottom for support.
2 While keeping the dog close to your body, so that he feels safe and secure and can't jump from your arms, stand up slowly.
3 Carry the dog close to your chest. To put him down, simply reverse the actions. Throughout, bend from your knees to avoid straining your back.

What is the best way to reprimand a dog when he's naughty?

The same principles apply to adult dogs as to puppies (see page 66). Teach only desirable behaviours and be consistent on a daily basis to avoid undesirable behaviours developing. Allowing your dog to jump on the sofa one day and not letting him the next will confuse him; either do or don't, but be consistent – then he knows where he is.

Avoid putting or allowing him in situations where he inadvertently gets things (in your view) wrong. For example, don't put the cat's food down where he can get at and eat it, or allow him to charge up or down stairs before you.

Physically punishing your dog indicates that you lack self-discipline and are too lazy to learn correct disciplinary techniques.

How can I tell if my dog has fleas?

Fleas live on the skin and in the coat of the host animal. Their scurrying about and biting in order to feed on their host's blood causes irritation, so if your dog is constantly scratching and biting at his coat, suspect fleas. Most active in warm, humid weather, you will see fleas (tiny black 'bugs') on the dog if you examine him closely.

Another way to check for fleas is to comb through the coat onto a damp piece of blotting paper – flea faeces turn rusty-red on the paper. See page 172 for details on treating your dog for fleas.

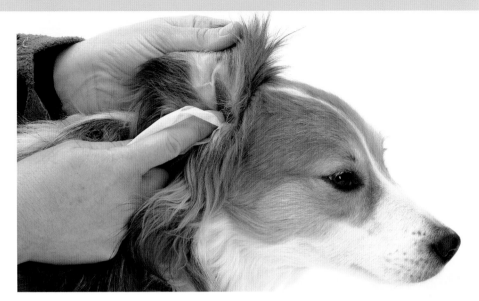

ABOVE Use ear wipes or cotton wool moistened with a small amount of canine ear cleaner to clean out the insides of your dog's ears gently. Never push the wipe or cotton wool further than it will go before it meets resistance.

RIGHT Dewclaws rarely raise cause for concern in pet dogs. If, however, dogs are frequently exercised through heavy ground cover there is a small chance that dewclaws could become caught on tough, trailing vegetation, and tear.

My dog's ears look dirty inside and he scratches at them often. Should I clean them out?

First, take your dog to the vet to check that he is not suffering from ear mites or an ear infection. If the ears are healthy but merely dirty, ask your vet for a proprietary product with which to clean them and get him to show you how to do this.

A healthy ear is pale pink and shiny inside, without discharge or wax.

Should my very active German Shepherd's dewclaws be removed?

Unless they cause a problem, it is better to leave dewclaws *in situ*. Dewclaws are rudimentary inner toes positioned on the lower leg rather than the paws and serve no useful purpose. Removing them from adult dogs is a major operation, with considerable discomfort for the dog during the healing process. As the wound site is in an easily accessible position, preventing the dog from worrying and licking at it (thereby delaying healing) creates a further problem.

My friend's vet has to empty her dog's anal sacs regularly. Why is this?

The anal sacs comprise sacs lined with cells that secrete a light brown, smelly-scented, oily liquid into the sacs. A small amount of this fluid is discharged when the dog defecates, leaving the dog's own scent message on his droppings.

If the liquid in the sacs thickens for some reason, it becomes more difficult to discharge and the sacs overfill, eventually becoming impacted and causing irritation and/or pain. When this happens, the sacs must be emptied manually. Suspect problems with the anal sacs if your dog starts paying increased attention to his bottom, or dragging it along the ground.

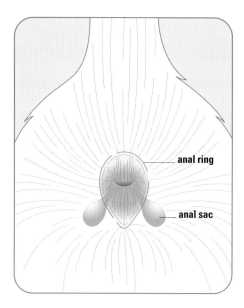

anal ring

anal sac

ABOVE The two anal sacs are situated on either side of the anus and secrete a fluid each time the dog defecates.

Can I give my dog aspirin or paracetamol tablets to ease the pain of his arthritis?

No – it is unsafe to give medication designed for humans to pets. Consult your vet as to which painkillers formulated for canines would be most suitable to ease your dog's pain. It is also worth consulting a holistic vet to enquire whether any of the many complementary therapies might be worth trying.

How can I keep my long-haired dog's back end clean?

It's important to keep your dog's undertail area clean, so that his faeces do not stick to his 'trousers'. This is essential in warm weather, both for the sake of hygiene and to reduce the risk of infection or maggot infestation.

Using a coat conditioner or gloss specially formulated for dogs on these areas will also help to prevent faeces sticking to the hair, or at least make it easier to wash off.

How will I know if my dog has worms?

'Scooting' is often an indication of worm infestation. This is when the dog drags himself along on his bottom in an effort to alleviate anal itching. You can sometimes see segments of tapeworms stuck to the fur around the dog's bottom (they look like grains of rice), while roundworms (resembling white threads) can be seen in the faeces. Heavily infested dogs may vomit worms. For details of how to treat for worms, see page 172.

What should I do if my dog goes missing?

Report your pet's disappearance to the police in case he's been found and handed in. Contact local authorities to see if any dogs have been reported killed or injured on the roads. Contact local vets and animal rescue centres. Ask neighbours if they have seen him, or will keep an eye out for him, and to check their property and outbuildings to see if he's trapped inside. Check vacant properties and garages, and find out if any neighbour has moved recently – sometimes dogs investigate removal wagons and inadvertently end up 'relocating' too.

Put up posters in local shops featuring a recent photo and a good description of your dog. Offering a reward helps. It's worth registering your dog on a 'lost and found' pet website.

BELOW The easiest way to help prevent hair soiling is to trim or clip excess hair from around your dog's anus and from his 'trousers'.

Despite regular training classes, I'm unable to cope with my dog. What should I do?

There are occasions when despite your best efforts, a partnership does not work. In these circumstances, it's more beneficial for both parties if you rehome the dog rather than persevere, with both of you frustrated and miserable.

Finding your pet a home with someone who can offer the type of environment, attention and training he needs is not a failure on your part, and does not imply that you are a bad owner. Rather, it is a selfless act that offers the dog a chance to lead a happier life with someone who is able to fulfil his needs.

Just because you have had to rehome your pet does not mean that you will be unsuccessful with another – make sure you choose your next dog more carefully.

ABOVE To rehome your pet, you could try advertising him and vetting prospective owners to satisfy yourself that they will offer a suitable home.

So how can I find the best possible home for him?

The breeder of your dog should be the first person you go to for advice. If they are unable to help, then dog rescue centres may be able to provide information. Some will even rehome him for you, provided you give them a donation to cover his keep until they do so. Alternatively, ask your vet and dog trainer if they know of an ideal home for your dog.

If your dog is a pedigree, find out if there is a 'breed rescue' in your area – your vet or trainer may know of one, or you could contact the breed organization for details.

Is it all right to keep a dog tied up in the garden at night as a watchdog?

Provided your dog has been trained to be tied up in such a way and is content with this, it should be fine. You will need to provide him with a warm, waterproof kennel in which to shelter and sleep. Place this just inside the limit of the tie line, so that he cannot wind the line around it and restrict his movement or even throttle himself. Provide him with clean, fresh water in a container that cannot be tipped over easily.

Make sure your dog's collar is comfortable and not too tight (you should be able to fit two fingers underneath it). Never attach a fixed line to a 'choke' collar, or your pet could strangle himself. Clear the area of any objects he could become caught up on.

Ensure that your boundary clearly displays 'Dog on guard' to warn people that he is there.

Is it all right to let a dog roam free outside while we're out at work?

This is definitely not a good idea due to the many risks involved. The dog could be injured on the road, cause traffic and other accidents, injure or terrorize people and other animals or vice versa, or be stolen. He is also vulnerable to contracting diseases or ingesting a harmful substance.

If the dog does cause harm to people, other animals or property, then you, as the owner, can be sued.

I'm worried that a neighbour's dog is not being looked after properly. What can I do?

It is better not to become directly involved yourself in case an unpleasant confrontation develops. The best thing to do is to contact a rescue organization – you do not have to give your name or address – and report your concerns. They will investigate and deal with the situation appropriately.

BELOW **Dogs found roaming unattended can be impounded by local authorities.**

4

Behaviour

How can I interpret what mood my dog is in?

Once you get to know your dog well, you will be able to recognize his moods. They will show in his body language, posture, facial and vocal expressions, and behaviour (see page 105). Just like humans, dogs experience moods of happiness, depression, frustration, contentment, anxiety, fear, anger and aggression. It is up to each owner to learn to recognize their pet's moods in order to be able to ascertain how he is feeling, what he wants and what he needs, in order to provide him with an improved quality of life.

ABOVE Many owners talk to their dogs and sometimes the two parties appear to understand each other.

How can I understand what my dog is 'saying'?

Dogs possess a large universal 'vocabulary' of vocal and physical expression. Generally, you can tell from the way a dog carries himself and acts what message he wants to convey. Examples are given in the table opposite.

How can I tell if my dog is happy?

A happy dog is confident, calm and relaxed. He looks well in himself, has a good appetite, doesn't constantly seek attention from his owner, has no behaviour problems and generally looks a picture of health.

Dogs have different personalities. While one happy dog may be playful, energetic and curious, another, equally happy, may be more laid-back, quiet and not as energetic. Learning how to interpret canine behaviour will enable you to judge a dog's state of mind.

How can I tell if a dog likes me?

If a dog likes you he will display several behaviours. He will be relaxed in your company, receive attention from you, and be willing to interact if you initiate contact or play. If he doesn't like you, he will be wary of you and avoid you.

Some dogs will show their dislike or unease by growling and assuming a threatening posture that says 'Don't come near me or I'll be forced to repel you.'

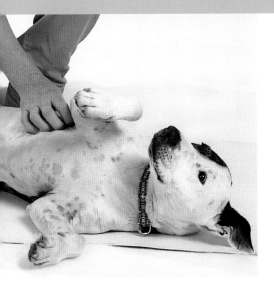

How can I tell if my dog is unhappy? What would make him so?

A dog will show his unhappiness through his behaviour, posture and, sometimes, vocal sounds. An unhappy dog will withdraw into himself; he may also develop what you consider undesirable behaviours, such as stereotypies (obsessive behaviours), in an effort to comfort himself.

In the same way as humans, some dogs become stressed by the hectic pace of their owners' lives. Busy owners tend to have too little time to meet their dog's

ABOVE If he likes a person, a dog will be eager to please and willing to do anything for them.

DOG 'VOCABULARY'

EMOTION	VISIBLE SIGNS
Aggression, fear and/or uncertainty	Stiff stance with jerky movements, growling, tail tucked between legs, snarling.
At ease	Relaxed posture, smooth movements.
Calm and alert	Pricked ears and kind, interested expression.
Frightened	Hunched up, ears down, cowed expression, growling or whining.
Curious, on guard and/or ready to spring into action	Intensely watchful.
Unhappy or ill	Stiff posture, ears down, slow movement.
On guard and ready to attack if necessary	Hackles raised, legs stiff, eyes fixed on subject, growling.
Submissive	Crouching, licking lips, whining.
Playful/happy/attention-seeking	Relaxed body and tail wag, 'smiley' face, lolling ears, excited yapping/barking.

needs, and fail to realize that actions or a tone of voice conveying impatience with their pet will wound him deeply, causing unhappiness.

Knowing your own dog's personality is the key to recognizing his emotional state at any given moment. Responding accordingly is the secret to happiness.

Why do dogs wag their tails?

A wagging tail does not necessarily mean that a dog is happy and friendly. The way in which the tail is wagged, along with the rest of the dog's body language, must be taken into account to ascertain whether he is a potential friend or foe.

HOW CAN I TELL THE DIFFERENCE BETWEEN AN AGGRESSIVE DOG AND A FRIGHTENED ONE?

The two will look and behave quite differently. The photographs below demonstrate these differences quite clearly.

ABOVE A frightened dog will cower and try to get away from whatever has scared him. He'll flatten his ears and tuck his tail between his legs, to keep these vulnerable body parts out of harm's way, and, with eyes wide, watch the threat intently for signs that he needs to flee quickly. He will look around him for the best and quickest means of escape. His body will be tense, even shaking, with his heart beating fast and adrenalin flowing, ready for a fast getaway.

ABOVE An aggressive dog will take up the stance of being 'armed to attack', with hackles raised (to make him appear bigger and more threatening), eyes fixed on his 'opponent', lips drawn back over the teeth ready to bite, and snarling/growling with intent. Some dogs remain, ominously, silent before they attack.

When I get over-stressed my dog becomes irritable and disobedient. How can I resolve this?

Dogs are quick to sense their owners' emotions. When all is not well they can become upset. Your pet's irritability and perceived disobedience is his way of protecting himself against the threat you pose to him when you are in a bad mood. In such a state, you are more likely to shout at him (dogs have extremely sensitive hearing and shouting at them causes physical discomfort) or even hit him, so it's not surprising he won't, for example, obey your order to come to you. Would you go to someone you think is going to shout at or attack you?

If you are in a bad mood, then wait until you have calmed down/cheered up before interacting with your pet. You will then find he'll respond to you better and

WHY DO SOME DOGS CHASE THEIR TAILS?

Tail-chasing is classed as a stereotypy (see page 105). It gives a needy dog something to do, providing a kind of comfort.

be happier in himself. A calm, contented and happy owner usually results in a dog that is likewise.

Why do dogs sniff each other's rear ends?

While humans use their eyes and hands to find out about the world around them, dogs use their noses and mouths. Sniffing other dogs' backsides, and also

TYPES OF TAIL-WAGGING

MOTION	EMOTION
Wagging a raised, stiff tail	Implies tension and potential aggression.
Wagging a low tail, possibly between his legs	Indicates fear and/or submission.
Energetically wagging a tail at half-mast	Usually a good sign.
Wagging with a relaxed body, 'smiley' face and lolling ears	Looking to play or receive attention.

faeces, the ground and other objects is an important part of canine interaction and communication.

By sniffing the ground, dogs can identify territorial boundaries and mating possibilities. Investigating another dog's rear end identifies its sex and whether it is a potential friend, mate or foe.

Why does my dog sniff visitors' groins, and how can I stop him?

Dogs sniff human crotches for the same reason they sniff other dogs' backsides (see page 107). Some dogs, especially males, are more persistent at doing this than others. This is particularly true of

ABOVE A special organ in the roof of the mouth (called the vomeronasal or Jacobson's organ) 'tastes' certain smells to help the dog analyze and react to them faster.

those who are tall enough for their heads to be, unfortunately, at crotch height, as this is the first part of the human with which the dog comes into contact.

The best way of dealing with this natural, but unacceptable, behaviour is to teach him to sit and stay when visitors call. He should wait until he's invited to greet them, and then sit by their side; stop him in his tracks if he makes a beeline for their nether regions by training him to respond to the command 'No'. See Chapter 5 for tips on training your dog.

Why does my dog bark at people who come to the door?

Your dog views your home and garden as his 'pack's' territory. For this reason, he will sound the alarm by barking when non-pack members intrude into his/your space.

While you want your dog to alert you to unwanted visitors, his barking at every person who comes to the door, such as regular delivery people, or who walks past the house can become a real nuisance. Introducing your dog to milk and post delivery people will teach him that they are 'friends' not 'foes' (getting them to give him treats is a good idea) and may help to cure the problem. See page 110 for advice on how to teach your dog to refrain from 'blanket barking'.

How can I stop my dog ripping up anything that comes through the letterbox?

By far the easiest and quickest way of dealing with your dog's penchant for eating the post is to provide a physical barrier. Fix a box under the letterbox on the inside of the door to catch mail as it is pushed through, or position a weatherproof, lockable postbox by the door on the outside (or in the open porch if you have one). Problem solved.

RIGHT **Barking is a dog's way of warning off perceived intruders.**

LEFT It's important to teach a dog from an early age to relinquish items without a fuss, otherwise he'll become a liability.

How can I stop my dog barking at anyone who walks past the house?

The reasons why your dog does this are explained on page 109. However, some breeds and types are more vocal in this respect than others, so if you live in a highly populated area bear this in mind when choosing a dog.

If your dog is left alone during the day, he could be barking at passers-by to give him something to do and to provide himself with a sense of security. If the problem is such that it is causing neighbours to complain (and this is understandable), then keep your dog out of rooms where he can see passers-by outside, and out of the garden at peak pedestrian times, to help alleviate the problem. Putting up a higher fence that he cannot see through can help, as it is usually the visual aspect that triggers the barking.

Teach your dog that barking at anything and everything (blanket barking) is unrewarding. When he barks, put him out of the room, or bring him indoors, and totally ignore him. When he's quiet, give him attention or a treat, and put him back *in situ*. He'll soon learn that barking is not as rewarding as being quiet, so will not bother. Giving him activity toys to keep him occupied will help keep him quiet, as will ensuring he receives enough attention and exercise.

Why does my dog guard his toys?

This is a natural canine behaviour. Being possessive about a toy or food, by growling threateningly or snapping at anyone who approaches to take it away, is a dog's way of saying 'it's mine and you can't have it', but this behaviour is inappropriate in a human environment.

If you teach your dog that relinquishing items, such as toys or food, earns him a reward – perhaps a treat, higher-value toy (see page 93) or lavish praise and attention – he'll learn that possessiveness is unrewarding and giving things to you, or allowing you to take them from him, is much more pleasant.

Rather than risk a confrontation, don't take toys from your dog – wait until he leaves them, then remove them if necessary.

Why does my dog howl when I go out, and how can I stop him?

Your dog is calling to locate his pack (his human family) and summon them back home. Being highly social animals, most dogs dislike being on their own because they feel insecure. It can sometimes help to give a rescue remedy – a solution of flower essences with calming and relaxing properties, available from health food shops.

Leaving suitable activity toys to keep your pet occupied while you are out can help, as can leaving a radio on to provide low background noise to soothe and comfort him. If this doesn't help, and his howling is causing a noise nuisance, then to negate the problem you will have to consider hiring a dog-sitter – see page 184 for various options.

Why does my dog bark at strangers when out on walks?

Your dog is protecting you and himself by warning off what he perceives as potential aggressors. It's a natural behaviour, but unacceptable in a human environment. Your dog has not been socialized adequately with other people, so he treats them all as 'foes' when out of the safety of his home environment.

RIGHT In situations like this, owners invariably become tense or try to reassure their pet, which simply reinforces the dog's view that there is something to be worried or defensive about, thereby making his behaviour worse.

The best way of overcoming this overprotective behaviour is to take him to socialization/training classes on a regular basis, where he'll meet other people and dogs in a controlled environment and learn to relax in their company.

Why does my dog bark and growl at other dogs he meets?

Usually this type of behaviour indicates fear and is therefore a defence strategy. It is also a sign of lack of socialization with other dogs, or sometimes a result of the dog being attacked by another at some point so that he has become wary of all dogs.

Whatever the reason for it, this behaviour is difficult to cure without expert help, so it pays to find a good dog trainer who can advise on the best course of action. Some trainers have their own friendly, trained dogs to help out in such situations and this often proves a real help, so try to find one who offers this service.

Why does my dog eat any animal dung he may find while out on walks?

Known as coprophagy (and sometimes, incorrectly, pica), this is quite common in dogs, although it seems disgusting to us. Other animals utilize food differently from dogs, so their faeces contain nutrients that the dog finds palatable or that his body craves.

Dogs usually come to no harm from eating faeces, but the habit can lead to illness should they ingest droppings that contain viruses, parasites or anthelmintics (de-worming products).

How can I stop my dog's revolting habit of eating animal faeces?

As your dog's instinct tells him that eating faeces is natural and acceptable, you should not become annoyed with him for doing so. Instead, discourage the habit by replacing it with a more acceptable alternative.

First, teach your pet to obey the command 'leave', rewarding him when he does so and comes to you; this also

ABOVE LEFT If they get the opportunity, most dogs will eat other animal's droppings.

ABOVE Rolling in dung and dead creatures is another undesirable canine habit. It is thought that a dog does this to disguise his scent while hunting, or to mark a stronger scent than his own on 'his' territory.

shows him that coming to you is far more rewarding than eating any droppings he's found. In persistent cases, muzzling your dog while out on walks will make it impossible for him to practise the habit.

Make sure that your dog's diet supplies all the nutrients he needs, then he won't feel the need to eat droppings to satisfy a nutritional deficiency.

My Jack Russell Terrier recently killed a garden bird. Why did he do this and how can I stop him doing it again?

Although this must have been distressing for you, it is important not to get angry with your pet. To him, this was a natural instinct to catch and despatch; terriers were originally bred to hunt and kill creatures (in your breed's case, specifically rats and mice).

The chances are that this was a one-off incident, as dogs rarely get the opportunity to catch birds unless they are the flightless variety, so it is unlikely it will happen again. If you feed birds, put food on a high bird table in a clearing, so that avian visitors have plenty of warning if predators are about.

My dog whines and waits by the door when my partner is almost home from work. How can he tell?

This phenomenon is not uncommon in dogs. Canine 'sixth sense' – a supposed intuitive facility, giving awareness inexplicable in terms of normal perception (extra-sensory perception/ESP) – is truly amazing.

Studies of dogs that appear to know when their owners are coming home have provided strong evidence of telepathy (distant feeling) between them. The idea that the dog simply got used to the routine of someone arriving home each day was disproved when dogs anticipated people arriving home at unexpected times. Also blown out of the water when tested was the theory that the dog picked up anticipatory vibes from someone at

home expecting a family member to come home. Hearing and smell were similarly discounted after tests.

The existence of a sixth sense still has to be proved scientifically, if it ever can be; until then, this behaviour remains a real and fascinating mystery.

How can I stop my dog chasing cats? He ignores 'leave' and recall commands.

In some dogs, the chase response is very strong. In these cases it can be extremely difficult, if not impossible, to cure the habit. Discuss the problem with a trainer to see if they can offer you a suitable training programme. The expert use of training discs or spray collars can prove effective in some cases, as they teach the dog that chasing after other animals is an unrewarding activity.

RIGHT **Most dogs are fine with their own cats, but will chase strange ones who stray into their garden or which they meet on walks. Muzzling a confirmed chaser when out walking will prevent him from getting hold of a cat should he catch up with one.**

My male 14-month-old German Shepherd still squats to urinate, like a bitch. Shouldn't he be lifting a leg by now?

Lifting a hindleg to urinate is the action of a mature, confident male dog. It's worth taking your pet to the vet to check that there is nothing wrong with his back or legs that would cause him to squat while urinating. If he gets the all-clear, then there is nothing to worry about – some dogs, especially large breeds, take longer to mature than others.

My two dogs fight a lot, as if each is trying to be 'boss'. How can I stop them?

Dogs sort out a natural pack hierarchy between themselves and it is important to support this. Favouring the dominant dog over the other will help to achieve an equable balance – for example, feed and give attention to the dominant dog

BELOW If in-fighting becomes severe it can be better for all concerned to rehome one of the dogs before one gets really hurt.

first. Remove items, such as toys and bones, that they are likely to have disputes over, and ensure both have their own bed and personal space to retire to.

If the dogs are both of the same sex, it can help to have one neutered.

How can I stop my dog jumping up at people?

First, never encourage your dog to jump up at you, as this simply reinforces the behaviour. If he does so, fold your arms and turn your head away from him, avoiding eye contact. Ignore him until he gets down – which he will when he fails to gain a response from you. Reward him when he has all four feet on the ground and makes no further attempt to jump up; this teaches him that jumping up is a negative experience, while not doing so is a positive one.

Our 3-year-old dog has become increasingly bossy and can threaten to bite. What can we do?

The problem here is that you have let your dog have his own way for too long. He now considers himself the pack leader – the most important member of your household. As you and your family are now frightened of your pet, you will find it difficult to cure the problem, even with expert help, as your confidence level around him is low.

In this case, it would be better to consider rehoming your dog before an

accident occurs. If you get another one, it will benefit you and other family members to take him to training classes from the start, so that you all learn how to handle him properly.

It's also worth having your vet check your pet before taking drastic action in case an ailment or an undetected injury is causing the behaviour.

BELOW Only give your dog attention when you have called him to you – never give it when he demands it, as this encourages attention-seeking behaviour, such as jumping up.

Why do the hairs on my dog's neck stand up when he's guarding something or sees another dog?

Raising the hackles (erectile hairs on the back of the neck and along the back) happens when the dog is alarmed or angry. The effect is to make the dog look bigger and therefore more threatening to potential aggressors.

My young cat got on well with our last dog who died recently. How can I introduce a new dog safely?

It would be better to introduce a puppy into the household than an adult dog. This is because a puppy is likely to be more accepting of existing pets and regard them as being higher up in the pack hierarchy than him. Your cat will also view a puppy as less of threat than an adult dog and be more relaxed about the newcomer.

My recently acquired young rescue dog is terrified of everyone and everything. How can I rebuild his confidence?

It sounds as though your dog has been inadequately socialized and/or mistreated. If he loves food, then this is the key to successful integration and training, although it is likely to be a long, slow process. Offering smelly, tasty treats will teach him that people can be rewarding; as he gains trust in coming to you for them (greed overcoming wariness), you can begin to handle him and train him to obey commands such as 'here'.

BELOW LEFT Muscles in the dermis (lower skin layer) control the movement of hairs on the surface of the skin. By lengthening and contracting them, a dog can raise his hackles.

BELOW Having the newcomer in a crate is a good way of introducing pets without the risk of inappropriate physical contact on either part.

ABOVE **Children who grow up with pets and are taught to treat them with respect and care are more likely to do better at school and develop into well-balanced and responsible adults.**

Joining a socialization/training class will help, but choose one carefully so as not to expose your dog to more than he can cope with. Insecure dogs quickly gain confidence if they have a 'sanctuary' within the home to which they can retire when things become too much for them (see pages 83–84). Giving him a rescue remedy (see pages 169–70) may help – consult a holistic vet.

How can I ensure that our dog does not nip the children while playing with them?

Do not leave your children with the dog unsupervised. They may tease him beyond endurance or play games that can get out of hand, causing the dog to become overexcited, and perhaps resulting in him nipping them.

Teach your children to respect their pet, and how to handle, speak to and play with him correctly. Taking them with you when you and the dog go to training/handling classes is a good idea in this respect.

How can I make sure other dogs don't attack mine while we're out walking?

You may be worrying about something that might never happen. Short of buying a house with plenty of private land on which to exercise your pet, you are bound to meet up with other dogs sooner or later. Provided your dog is well trained, will recall immediately, is under control on and off the leash, and is non-reactive towards other dogs, the chances of other dogs attacking him are slight.

Anxious owners transfer their anxieties to their dogs, making them more likely to be negatively reactive with other people and animals. It would benefit you both to attend a regular training/socialization class in order to lean how to cope in canine company.

My dog is confrontational with other dogs. Should I muzzle him when I take him out?

It's possible that your pet is fearful of other dogs, so uses aggression to try to make them go away from him. However, this tactic can backfire when another dog accepts the challenge.

In the short term, muzzling him will prevent him from biting another dog, although bear in mind that he won't be able to defend himself should the roles be reversed and another dog attacks him.

To effect a long-term cure, enrol in a dog training class to learn how to handle your dog better in all respects, and to train and socialize your pet.

Why does my dog urinate whenever I pick her up or when other dogs or people come near her?

Urinating like this is usually a symptom of fear or excitement. The extreme emotion results in the bladder sphincter muscle relaxing, allowing urine to be passed unintentionally. Taking your dog to training/socialization classes will help to boost her confidence in company or calm her down, thus alleviating or even solving the problem.

Take your dog to the vet to check that the cause is not an ailment or infection; one potential cause is a bladder sphincter muscle weakness, which causes a condition known as urethral sphincter mechanism incompetence (USMI). In this case the prognosis is good, as it usually responds well to medication.

Why does my dog stop frequently while out on a walk to urinate against lamp posts and vehicle tyres?

Urinating against objects and/or defecating on or next to other dogs' droppings is a highly effective messaging service. The scent left behind in this 'calling card' tells other dogs who will be passing that way, what sex your dog is and how big he is – hence the reason for male dogs aiming to leave their urine, and often their faeces, as high as possible. It is perfectly normal canine behaviour; other pack animals such as wolves use this system to mark territory.

How can I stop my dog soiling in the house?

If your dog has not been adequately house-trained, then he is likely to soil inside. Do not punish him, as he won't understand why you are doing so and the stress of you being cross with him will probably make the problem worse. For house-training tips, see pages 64–65.

Do you leave your dog alone for long periods, for which it is unreasonable to expect him to 'hold on'? If so, arrange for someone to let him out during that time to toilet. Get to know when he usually eliminates, such as after a meal, and aim to let him out around this time.

ABOVE Urinating to leave a scent message for other dogs is known as 'marking'.

BELOW If they are stressed about something or feel unwell, some dogs will uncharacteristically soil in the house.

How do I stop my dog trying to 'mate' people's legs, cushions and soft toys?

Owners can find this behaviour embarrassing, but to a dog it is a natural activity. Both sexes will display this 'inappropriate sexual behaviour', often as they are maturing. It can represent experimentation with sex, a dominant behaviour or a sign of insecurity – the dog trying to convince himself he's in charge.

Young dogs normally grow out of this behaviour; neutering may help. If he's an established adult, then the best way of dealing with it is to ignore it. If none of these solutions works, seek advice from your vet and/or a canine behaviourist.

If your dog embarrasses visitors, distract him with a toy or put him out of the room.

ABOVE A new dog or puppy may settle better if allowed to sleep in your room for a night or two.

Is it all right to let my dog sleep on the bed?

Many people do let their dog(s) sleep on their bed and find it a great comfort. However, you should be aware of the health and safety reasons why it isn't such a great idea.

● There is the potential for your dog to deposit fleas and shed hair on your bed, both of which are likely to cause skin irritation to humans.

● The dog may consider himself your equal by being allowed to sleep on your bed and this may lead him to challenge your leadership. As a result you may have discipline problems.

● Some dogs don't appreciate being disturbed when they are asleep or having to move from a comfy spot, resulting in a confrontation.

How can I stop my dog jumping onto the sofa and my bed?

To keep your dog off furniture when you cannot monitor him, restrict his access to the sitting room and bedroom. You can simply close the doors, or use a stair gate or obstacles. If he tries to jump up when you are there, say 'No!' and make sure he obeys.

If you see him on the furniture, insist that he gets off; if he won't, hook your finger under his collar and firmly remove him. If he tries to get back up, say 'No';

ABOVE Replacing a see-through fence with a solid one can help alleviate quarrelling between neighbouring dogs.

put him out of the room if necessary. He'll learn that it's more rewarding to stay off the furniture (he can stay in the room) than jump on it. Make sure all members of the family adhere to the rules.

Sometimes my dog furiously scratches the carpet. Why?

It is likely that he is simply 'making a bed'. If he lies down on the spot where he has been scratching, this confirms it.

If your dog's paws are sore or itchy, he may be doing this to alleviate discomfort. If the scratching becomes a regular occurrence, take him to the vet to have this possibility checked.

If there is an air space under the floor, it could be harbouring animals such as rats or mice. Your dog knows they are there, hence his scratching – he's trying to get at them.

My dog and my neighbours' dog bark furiously at each other through the garden fence. How can we stop them?

Why don't you consider taking both dogs to a training class? The two dogs can then meet and integrate in a controlled environment, with an expert on hand to help and advise. Follow this up by taking the dogs out for walks together and playing games with them, in an effort to help them become friendly.

If none of this works, then avoid letting out the dogs at the same time. Consult your neighbour to arrange mutually convenient staggered times.

Why do dogs lick their backsides and how can I stop my pet doing this?

Few owners enjoy the sight of a dog using his tongue to clean his private places. However, this practice is an essential and effective part of attending to his personal hygiene. If you find it abhorrent, then go out of the room until he's finished, or distract him into doing something else but never tell him off as he will not understand why you are doing so.

Why does my dog take dirty washing out of the laundry basket, and how can I stop him?

Your dirty laundry is rich in the smells of members of the family. Your pet is probably taking them for comfort or to sniff through them at his leisure. Either put the laundry basket somewhere where your dog cannot get at it, or invest in one with a lid he cannot remove.

Why does my dog scavenge in the kitchen waste bin if he gets the chance?

Dogs retain the innate drives of their ancestors, one of which was to scavenge for food. It's a natural behaviour, but in most cases they can be taught not to raid the bin. If you have a scavenger, the simplest solution is to ensure the bin is not accessible to your pet.

BELOW LEFT When scavenging in bins, dogs are at risk from cutting themselves on glass or cans, and also from digestive upsets by eating unsuitable items.

BELOW Left to their own devices in the big wide world, dogs can be cunning thieves with an eye for a good opportunity.

How can I stop my dog thieving things from the street or people's gardens?

Your dog should not be allowed to roam at will on the streets(see page 101). Not allowing him outside on his own will solve the problem.

Why does my dog chew his toys to bits?

Playing with toys fulfils a dog's natural desires to hunt, chase, kill and eat his prey. Chewing up his toys combines the latter two actions. Chewing toys also helps to keep his gums and teeth in good condition.

BELOW **If your dog shreds his toys, choose more durable ones made from hard rubber or plastic. They may be more expensive, but are ultimately cost-effective (see pages 46–47).**

Why do dogs eat grass?

Eating grass aids the dog's digestion. This habit is known as 'pica' – a tendency or craving to eat substances other than normal food, in this case occurring as a symptom of disease. When dogs feel ill, they eat grass to induce vomiting and rid the stomach of whatever disagrees with them. Excessive grass-eating should be investigated by your vet, as it may indicate a serious digestive problem.

My dog has a constant supply of fresh, clean water, so why does he drink from dirty puddles?

Water is water to a dog, dirty or not – they are not generally fussy. While many dogs do not suffer ill-effects from drinking from puddles and other outside sources, it is not wise to let them do so in case the water is contaminated, by either chemicals or parasites.

My dog drags his bottom along the floor. Why?

Dragging his bottom along the floor (scooting) indicates that your dog is suffering at his rear end. This could be due to:
- Worms (see page 98).
- Blocked anal glands (see page 98).
- Rectal irritation.

Take your dog to be examined by the vet, so that the appropriate treatment can be administered.

Why does my dog dig holes in the garden and how can I stop him?

Digging indicates that your dog is looking for food or for quarry to chase and catch. Hunting dogs and terriers are most prone to digging in areas that their sense of smell tells them will be rewarding, so unless you want your garden rearranged, reserve a special area in which your pet can indulge in this harmless habit.

Before lying down to rest or sleep, my dog turns round and round. Why?

This behaviour harks back to his wild ancestors. They were thought to adopt this action to tread down grass and

ABOVE If you bury a toy or bone in his special spot, your dog will get a reward for his efforts and keep returning to it to try his luck again, leaving the rest of the garden unspoiled.

ground cover to make a comfy bed to sleep on, and also to dislodge any creatures already inhabiting the area. The turning may also be accompanied by scratching at the bedding (see page 121).

Do dogs need the company of other dogs to remain contented and happy?

Some do, some don't – it depends on the nature of each individual. Generally, dogs are highly sociable and enjoy the company of other likewise friendly dogs, but some prefer to be the only canine member of the household.

Whenever my partner and I sit down together, our dog starts whining for our attention. Why?

ABOVE LEFT Two dogs that get on well together enjoy a close friendship – and you get twice the pleasure.

ABOVE It's safer for all concerned to put your dog outside in the garden or shut him in another room while you are vacuuming.

If your partner is a new one, then your dog may be being protective of you, unsure of your partner's intentions. If your partner is of long standing, then it sounds like a case of attention-seeking, especially if your dog is emotionally closer to one of you than the other.

In both cases, ignore your dog – shutting him in another room if necessary – when he displays this attention-seeking behaviour. Any kind of attention from you, whether to reassure the dog or physically/vocally send him away, will serve to reinforce your dog's unease in the former case, and be interpreted as a reward for his behaviour in the latter.

How can I stop my dog from chasing the vacuum cleaner ?

Your dog's body language will tell you what's going on. He either sees the vacuum cleaner as a monster that hurts his ears and is chasing it away, or considers it a highly enjoyable game.

If he's frightened, acclimatize him to it in a rewarding way so that he views it as non-threatening. Give him treats while you vacuum or his favourite toy to play with, but otherwise ignore him. If he's playing, discourage him from doing so.

Attention-seeking • Vacuum-attack **125**

Why does my dog eat our cat's faeces out of the litter tray and how can I stop him?

The reasons for this are discussed on page 112. The best way of dealing with it is to make the faeces inaccessible: position the tray where your cat can get at it, but not your dog.

Alternatively, a hooded litter tray can solve the problem – but only if your dog's head is too big for him to put it through the entrance.

BELOW **Programmes featuring animals tend to provoke intense canine curiosity.**

Our dog gets excited when he sees and hears animals on the TV. Can he see and understand what is happening?

Canine eyes are constructed differently to humans'. They cannot see as well as we can as far as colours and distance are concerned, although they are more sensitive to light and movement. It is likely that your dog is attracted to the moving images on the TV, as well as the sounds from it, rather than actually watching and understanding a programme. But it is possible that he is able to identify the sounds of other animals when he hears them on TV.

Is growling and lip-curling always a sign of aggression?

Together, these actions usually convey a warning to whoever is approaching the dog to back off. This is especially true if they are accompanied by a tense, watchful posture. On the other hand, some dogs display this behaviour as a sign of pleasure. Getting to know your dog well will help you to determine his mood when he uses these signals.

BELOW 'Grinning' can sometimes be mistaken for snarling but is a sign of submission, either when greeting people or when being admonished.

Why does my dog chase after cars and bicycles, and how can I stop him?

Some dogs have a very strong instinct (prey drive) to chase anything that moves. It can be very difficult to cure such a habit without expert help tailored to the individual. Successful training depends on what level of obedience training the dog is at and identifying what motivates him to chase certain things, in order to effect the best programme to (hopefully) solve the problem. The main areas to address are obedience on the 'leave' command, and also an immediate 'down' and recall response.

Find a trainer who can help you with this, and in the meantime keep your dog on a leash when in public places so he cannot chase after vehicles and risk causing an accident.

Why do dogs shake their bodies when they get wet?

This is a dog's instinctive reaction to rid the skin and coat of water so that it dries quickly. It helps to make him comfortable and less susceptible to ailments.

My dog 'shakes' his toys and growls. Why?

He's practising his hunting skills. In shaking and growling at the toy he is subduing it, as he would with live prey, before administering the killing bite. This is nothing to worry about – your pet gets a good deal of enjoyment from such behaviour with his toys.

My dog seems to be 'hyperactive'. How can I calm him down?

An overabundance of activity may simply be a young dog in high spirits, but could also be due to any of the following:
- Anxious owner transferring anxiety to the dog.
- Artificial ingredients, such as colourings, preservatives and other additives in the diet.
- Breed trait.
- Insufficient mental and/or physical exercise.

Addressing, identifying and eliminating the possible cause(s) for your dog's hyperactivity is the solution to your problem. A holistic vet and/or dog trainer will help you do this if necessary; the former may suggest natural relaxants for your dog. Try the following:

ABOVE **Raggers and soft toys are ideal toys for your pet to 'kill'.**

- Remain calm and unhurried.
- Change the diet – avoid any food or treats with artificial ingredients.
- Find out more about the breed and how best to handle/manage it. Contacting breeders is a good place to start, as is a canine behaviourist.
- Provide more exercise, physically and mentally – join a training/agility club.

Can a canine behaviourist help solve the problems I have with my dog, and what do they do?

A behaviourist will take a detailed account of your dog's history, your lifestyle and his behaviour. The more information you supply the better. In taking a comprehensive history and studying how you interact with him, the behaviourist will pinpoint the root of any problems you have and decide on the most appropriate way of dealing with them, within your capabilities.

In some cases there is no quick-fix solution to a problem, so be prepared for the process to be lengthy, often necessitating regular visits.

ABOVE **Vets and canine rescue centres are usually able to recommend a reputable canine behaviourist.**

5

Socializing and training

What does 'socialization' mean?

This term has two aspects to it. The first is that the dog is trained to mix socially with other creatures, and the second is that he behaves in a way that is acceptable in the society in which he lives – that is, within a household as a domestic pet.

In the wild, parents raise their puppies to adhere to a social code and respect the natural hierarchy within the pack. They are taught and quickly learn what comprises acceptable behaviour and what does not, in order to survive.

BELOW Dogs are naturally highly sociable creatures, but have to be taught how to be so.

In a domestic environment, once they leave their mother and siblings, puppies must be taught by their human 'parents' how to behave acceptably in human and dog company and how to cope with life in the human world.

How long does it take to socialize a dog?

If it is done properly and in a comprehensive manner, a young dog will be well socialized by the age of 9 months. However, he will always be seeing, meeting and experiencing new things, so socializing is really an ongoing process throughout his life.

What sorts of things does my dog need to learn to accept?

The answer is anything and everything. He needs to learn how to socialize with other dogs, be polite and calm when meeting people and other creatures, and learn when enough is enough during attention and play sessions.

Accustom your young dog to meeting and being with people of both sexes, all ages and different appearances, and reward him so that he views their company as a good thing. Handling him when he is eating and playing with toys will teach him not to become possessive about either.

When accustoming my dog to sights and sounds, how much should I do in one session?

Introduce your pet to things one at a time. Never present two things in one session as it will be too much for him to cope with mentally. To start with, one or two 10-minute sessions per day is enough. Be careful not to overwhelm your dog; take things at his pace.

Some areas of socialization may need more acclimatization that others, so be prepared for this and remember that time

and patience work wonders. Rushing the process can result in your pet becoming nervous and timid or even aggressive, or it could make existing problem behaviours even worse rather than alleviating them.

Make introductions to new things short and always rewarding, so that your dog views them as good experiences.

RIGHT Meeting traffic can be a frightening experience for a young dog as it's so big, fast and noisy. Start with a quiet road – show the pup a treat when a vehicle approaches and let him have the reward when it has gone past. This way he'll associate traffic with something nice not nasty.

What will happen if my dog is not socialized?

Different breeds/types of dogs will enjoy the company of people and other animals to different extents. However, all dogs like to live their lives in a pack, whether human or canine (or a bit of both). If denied social contact, dogs, like humans, can easily become depressed or 'badly behaved'.

Imagine a world where you cannot speak the language, are afraid of someone walking towards you on a street, or meeting a group of people terrifies you. Without realizing, you can turn a dog into a nervous wreck simply by not socializing him.

A dog can be a nightmare to live with, handle and control if he hasn't been socialized, so you need to do this properly for the safety and contentment of all concerned.

ABOVE Some training schools offer residential courses for livestock socialization training, which can be of great help.

Who can I turn to if I need help in socializing my dog?

A good dog trainer will be of great help in this respect. If you join a socializing class, it will give you and your dog the opportunity to meet other people and dogs, as well as a chance to learn how to cope with different situations and problems. You will also have on-the-spot expert advice when situations crop up in company that you are not sure how to deal with correctly.

If you have problems socializing your pet, it can be a good idea to consult a canine behaviourist (see page 129).

How can I get my dog used to other animals?

Some training schools hold introduction classes, where dogs have the chance to meet other animals. It is worth making the effort to get to such a class, as they tend to have more success than trying to do this yourself. The class offers a controlled environment with expert help if you need it. It will boost your confidence and feeling of control, which is essential for successful training.

You may have to travel some distance to find such a class, but making that effort should pay dividends.

ABOVE **Getting together with other dog owners locally for walks is a help in socializing dogs, provided they get on well together after initial introductions have been made.**

Despite socialization classes, my dog is not improving. Why – and how can we make any progress?

There could be several reasons for the lack of progress. Sometimes it is due to the owner not taking the dog to socialization classes as often as necessary (it should be at least weekly), or that they are not continuing the correct training at home between classes. Alternatively, it may be that the class you are attending does not suit you and/or your dog, so it might be worth trying a different trainer or class.

How can I stop my dog chasing after other dogs and livestock?

Many dogs find the experience of chasing animals very enjoyable and therefore rewarding. Curing a confirmed chaser can be extremely difficult and you will almost certainly not solve the problem without expert help, so the first thing you need to do is find a good training school in which to enrol.

Using a training disc can be particularly helpful in educating 'chasers', but you must be taught how to use it correctly or it will be worthless. It consists of a number of thin metal discs on a loop that you shake or drop on the ground when the dog performs the undesirable behaviour, to make a distinctive noise that the dog finds

unrewarding. This will eventually persuade him to refrain from chasing other animals, as he will not want to hear the noise.

In the meantime, keep your dog on the leash while out walking until the problem is solved.

ABOVE LEFT Using a long line enables the dog to run relatively freely, while the owner retains overall safe control of his movements.

ABOVE For safety's sake, use a stair gate to segregate a dog from people he is unsure of, without isolating him, so that he can become accustomed to them in his own time.

My dog growls at my grandchildren when they visit. How can I get him to accept them?

With any form of aggression, it's important to seek practical help from a dog trainer. Don't try to deal with the problem on your own as this rarely works. When people are at risk of being bitten it simply is not worth taking the chance.

Perhaps your dog has been tormented by the children previously, so is acting defensively, or they could be too loud for him. Until you get practical help, keep your pet safely out of the way when your grandchildren visit, and teach them how to behave appropriately around animals.

My dog doesn't actually chase our cat, but relentlessly follows her around. How can I stop him?

If the cat is not overly bothered by your dog's 'hounding' behaviour, this is a good sign. Cats that don't run won't trigger a dog's chase instinct. The chances are that when he gets too close for comfort, your cat will warn him off with a swipe or growl and he'll back off, as cats can make formidable adversaries.

The best way of dealing with this problem is to ensure your cat has plenty of escape routes in the house, such as shelves to jump up on, so that she can get out of the dog's way if she deems it necessary.

What does 'training a dog' comprise?

Training a dog consists of teaching him how to be a 'good citizen'. This means training him to be well-mannered and obedient, sociable, and safe to be around people, traffic and other animals.

Regular training – that is, reinforcement on a daily basis – ensures that bad habits don't creep in, and those that do are quickly cured. It will help make your dog a well-behaved member of society.

I want to compete in agility classes with my dog. Where do I start?

Join a dog training school that offers agility on its curriculum. To get the most out of the activity, and be successful at it, dogs must be obedience-trained first so that they respond to your commands and signals.

BELOW **Most dogs thoroughly enjoy agility activities and the interaction with the other humans and dogs taking part.**

Is there any special equipment I need for dog training?

Ideally, you should have a three-in-one training leash and a half-check collar (see pages 79–80), of appropriate length and size for your pet. In addition, a bumbag is useful for holding the food treats used for training purposes, as it saves your pockets becoming dirty and sticky.

Toys are useful motivators, so for training purposes choose those that your dog values most.

Where do I start in training my dog?

The first thing to understand is that successful training is based upon reward. Generally, dogs love to please their owners, and enjoy doing so even more when they are rewarded for it. Reward-based training is, therefore, the key to achieving a happy and obedient dog.

The second most important thing to realize is that for the best results you will need expert help in training your dog. It pays to look around for a trainer/training school that you feel can offer you and your dog the best tuition.

How will my dog understand what I'm telling him to do when I'm training him?

Your dog will learn to associate a word with an action. You must be aware of what both your tone of voice and body posture are telling him. For example, if you are encouraging the dog to come to you, you must ensure your body language is as welcoming as your voice.

Rewarding your dog every time he acts as you wish on a particular word-action command will lead to a learned response. Eventually, that response will become automatic every time you say the command.

Beware of unconsciously rewarding undesirable behaviour, otherwise your dog will assume his inappropriate actions are acceptable.

ABOVE Dog training classes, preferably weekly, but at least once a month, will help keep you and your dog on the right track.

RIGHT **Once you have the names of likely trainers, contact them to find out if they are able to help with your dog's education. Prepare a list of questions to ask beforehand.**

Do I have to take my dog to training classes or can I train him myself?

Without expert on-the-spot help and advice to guide you, this will be difficult. Unless you have dog-training experience, you may find it impossible to train a dog to an acceptable standard on your own. A trainer is immediately on hand to help you overcome any problems that crop up, and offer advice on alternative methods if the one you are using isn't producing the desired results.

You'll also get essential moral support from a trainer; going it alone can sap your confidence if you come up against a problem that gets worse rather than better.

How do I find a reputable trainer?

The best way to find a trainer is by word of mouth. Ask dog-owning friends which trainer they go to and quiz them about the methods used. Find out also if they feel able to relate to the trainer, as being able to talk to them is extremely important for your sense of wellbeing, which in turn will benefit your dog.

Your vet and local rescue kennels are another point of contact. Local telephone directories are another source, as is the internet.

What should I look for in a trainer?

Good trainers will:
- Ask for detailed information about your dog and whether he has had any training at all.
- Enquire what the problem is (if any) and what you want your dog and you to gain from training classes.

● Invite you to come along to a class or two, with or without your dog, and watch what goes on. This allows them to meet you and your dog before you book sessions. If they do not offer, ask – if you sense reluctance, it's sensible to take your custom elsewhere.

Small classes are preferable, so that the trainer retains control and everyone gets enough attention.

BELOW A sign of a good trainer/training class is that the owners and dogs are happy and enjoying themselves, and control is being exercised.

What should I expect from a training class?

On visiting a class prior to taking your dog, check that kind, albeit firm, training is implemented. If you spot any evidence of unkindness, cruelty, or anything else you would be unhappy subjecting your dog to, leave and go elsewhere.

Some trainers offer one-to-one tuition, although this is usually for 'problem' dogs in the first instance, so that the trainer can assess both owner and dog and judge the best way of progressing.

Ideally, classes should number no more than six dogs, so that the trainer can devote enough attention to each client. Any more than this, and more nervous dogs will feel overwhelmed.

Why has my trainer told me to get a check-choke or broad collar instead of a choke chain?

Used correctly in expert hands, choke (check) chains can be an effective training aid. Unfortunately, all too often they are used incorrectly by amateurs, and cause physical and mental damage. Put one around your own wrist and pull on it, and you'll feel the strangling effect it is capable of delivering.

The types of collars your trainer has suggested are 'kind' ones, in that they are the least likely to do any damage to your dog's neck should he pull or you inadvertently tug him while he is on the leash.

Are there any specific toys that are good for training?

Your dog will put a certain value on each of his toys, more on some than on others (see page 93). The ones he perceives as higher in value are the most useful for training – your dog will want them, so he can be persuaded to 'earn' them by displaying the behaviour you require.

RIGHT Using higher-value toys in training will encourage your dog to behave as you require.

Dogs tend to place a high value on squeaky, chase and ragger toys. Keep them as such by allowing your dog only limited access to them – that is, only when training.

What sort of training rewards are most suitable for a dog?

It depends whether your dog is food-, toy- or attention-orientated. If food is the key, then really smelly, tasty treats (such as cooked liver pieces and hot dog

exercise, interspersed with play sessions for light relief, until you have perfected it; then move on to the next task.

Puppies do not have a prolonged attention span: three 10-minute sessions a day are better than one 30-minute session.

sausage or soft chewy commercial treats) are excellent motivators. Some dogs prefer fresh fruit or vegetable treats. Cut treats into tiny pieces so they go further.

If your dog will do anything for attention, then vocal praise and gentle stroking (not patting, as this can be uncomfortable for a dog) comprise a reward. For toys, see page 93.

Remember: your dog has to earn the good thing he desires.

How many training sessions does a dog need, and how long should they last?

The key is little and often, always finishing on a good note. Reinforcing appropriate behaviour on a daily basis keeps the dog mannerly and under control. Sessions should last for as long as it takes for the dog to display the required behaviour (this can be minutes in some cases), but maintain them for no longer than 10–15 minutes of concentrated training in 1 hour. Aim to do one

How long does it take to train a dog to be obedient?

This depends on the character of the dog and his owner, and how adept they are as pupil and teacher. Some dogs learn faster than others, while some owners are simply not good teachers, lacking the control, self-restraint, willpower and technique required to teach their dogs manners and obedience.

Large breeds mature more slowly than smaller dogs, so you need to be extra patient. Smaller dogs can be too clever for their own good, so you have to be on your toes! Working breeds are intelligent and quick to learn, but also have a strong instinct to chase and retrieve, guard or herd – or all three – so require disciplined training to gain the best from them.

When is a dog fully trained?

Given the correct training, which is continually reinforced, it's possible to have a mentally well-balanced dog who is well-mannered and obedient in a matter of weeks. The training needs to

RIGHT Problem behaviours that have become ingrained are likely to take some time to overcome.

continue on a daily basis for him to remain so; you can never rest on your laurels, otherwise bad habits and undesirable behaviours tend to creep in undetected until they become a problem.

Continual reinforcement means that when you have taught your dog to do something, you must repeat the lesson often so that he does not forget how to respond to the given command.

All dogs are different, so some take longer to train than others, plus it very much depends on the ability of the owner.

When can I stop going to training classes?

When you think that you have achieved your desired standard of control. However, without regular training classes to keep you on your toes, it is very easy to become lazy where maintaining your dog's level of obedience is concerned. It's worth going to classes on an occasional basis, maybe once every month or so, to keep you both up to the required standard.

Is it a good idea to send a dog away to a training school?

In my view, no. This is because you are not there to check how well your dog is cared for and what methods are being used to train him – you may not approve of some of these. Bear in mind also that while your dog may respond to whoever was training him, he may not respond to you in the same way when he returns home from training school.

It is better for both you and your dog to be trained together at the same place.

Are there any residential training courses for myself and my dog?

Yes there are – these can be found via dog magazines and the internet. Vet them carefully as, like most things, some are better than others. Some specialize in particular areas, such as socializing dogs with livestock or agility training, while others provide a comprehensive curriculum of activities from which you can pick and choose.

What are the best ways of rewarding and reprimanding a dog while training him?

Rewards for good behaviour should be given instantly, so that your dog associates the behaviour with the reward. They can take the form of a food treat, a play session with or without a favourite toy, gentle attention or vocal praise. A reward can also be as simple as letting the dog back into the room when he's stopped barking.

Where reprimands are concerned, raising your voice and/or hitting a dog will simply confuse and frighten him, making him less receptive to learning the right way to do something. Ignoring the dog is a very effective reprimand when necessary, as is using something he doesn't associate with you to distract him from inappropriate behaviour – this could be a startling noise out of his line of vision. He'll associate the unpleasant noise with the behaviour, therefore find it unrewarding and so stop doing it.

Why are other people's dogs progressing faster than mine at our training class?

There are no set time limits on how long it should take for a dog's training to progress. In fact, setting time limits can be counterproductive if the owner thinks the dog is 'not progressing as he should'. The time it takes to achieve success depends on the aptitude of both dog and owner.

Have a word with the trainer, who may be able to set your mind at rest regarding your dog's progress, or even

BELOW Residential training schools can be great for intensive training courses, but you should not consider one residential visit to be the entirety of your dog's training.

suggest alternative methods that may work better for you both. As a last resort, try another training school to see if that suits you better.

Why does my dog behave better for my trainer than for me?

Your dog senses that the trainer is confident and experienced with dogs and so views that person as the pack leader. This being the case, he is more likely to respond well to the trainer. Don't worry, however, because as your confidence and experience develops and grows by going to training classes, you will gain the same respect from your dog, provided you handle him appropriately. His behaviour will improve accordingly.

I can't take my dog to a trainer; would they come to me?

Some trainers will come to owners' homes for one-to-one consultations and training sessions. It's a question of finding one (see page 139). A trainer will work with the facilities you have, so if these are limited it is not a problem. In some cases it can be beneficial for a dog to be trained at home, as the trainer can identify the causes of particular problems you may be having with your pet.

BELOW LEFT It's not always necessary to reward good behaviour with treats. Most dogs adore being rewarded with lavish praise from their owner.

BELOW Sometimes problems are most effectively resolved through one-to-one help from a trainer.

LEFT It is possible for disabled owners to take a well-trained dog for walks.

My dog does his best to get his collar off and won't move when on the leash. What should I do?

Ideally, your dog should be trained to his collar and leash as a puppy. Even if he is older, by following the training instructions on pages 58 and 59, you and your dog should soon be enjoying your walks. You could also try a different type of collar – a lighter one perhaps – and make sure it fits correctly so that it doesn't cause discomfort (see page 46).

I'm disabled – is it possible to train a dog to walk sensibly beside my mobility carriage?

Yes it is, although some dogs have more aptitude for this than others. It all depends on the type and temperament of your pet. You will need the help of a good trainer who has experience in such training to help you teach your pet to be steady, attentive to your commands and therefore safe to take out for walks beside your mobility carriage.

It would be worth your while contacting disabled organizations, and also dog training societies, to see if they can recommend a trainer. Otherwise, you will need to seek one out (see page 139).

How do you teach a dog to sit?

Four principles apply in teaching your dog to sit on command, and the acronym ACER will help you remember them:

- Attention
- Command
- Execute
- Reward

1 Stand with your dog by your side, with the leash and a treat in the same hand. Get his attention by saying his name.
2 Command 'sit' and simultaneously gently push his rear end down.
3 Responding to the pressure, your pet will execute the command by sitting.
4 When he does so, reward him with the treat.

How do I teach my dog to lie down on command?

There are three steps to follow:

1 With your pet in the sit position, get him to focus his attention on a treat (or toy) in your hand.

2 Put the treat under his nose so he can have a good sniff, then slowly move it down to the floor or between his front paws, whereupon he will sink to the floor in an effort to get it. As he does so, say 'down' and reward him.

3 Practise this a couple of times and you'll find your dog soon learns to lie down on command in anticipation of a reward.

ABOVE Always request that your dog sits before feeding him or putting him on the leash.

BELOW Only once your dog sits on command should you teach him to lie down.

How do I teach my dog to stay on command?

Follow steps 1–3 for the lie down (see page 147) then extend this into a stay:
1 Step away from the lying dog and firmly say 'stay'. Use a hand signal if necessary, which should comprise your hand pointing down, with either palm down or finger pointing down.
2 Wait a couple of seconds before going back to your pet and reward him lavishly.
3 Gradually extend the distance between you and your dog as you give the command to stay.

How do I train my dog to walk calmly to heel?

Begin the training exercise with your dog on your left-hand side. His shoulder should be against your leg and the leash held loosely across your body in your right hand. Then:
1 Say his name to get his attention, then say 'heel'.
2 Begin walking purposefully.
3 If your pet walks in front of you or pulls on his lead to get ahead of you, stop. He will no doubt look back at you in surprise.
4 Guide him back into position by your left-hand side, with his shoulder against your leg. Get his attention again, as in step 1. Begin walking again.
　Patiently repeat the steps as required and your pet will soon get the idea that staying at heel is rewarding (he gets to walk with you), while not doing so isn't rewarding (he has to stop).

I keep losing my dog's attention. How can I keep him focused on the training?

Dogs become bored very quickly if you practise the same exercise over and over. If you get a positive result on the first attempt, don't repeat the exercise. Finish on this good note with a play session.

BELOW Remember to use the command 'heel' only when your dog is in that position, so that he learns the word by association. Once he has learned where 'heel' is, you can use the command to return him to that position.

The clever use of training toys and treats will also help keep your dog's attention where you want it – on you. Remember to reward him whenever he offers a desired behaviour, as this keeps his motivation high.

How can I teach my dog to travel well?

Basic information on transporting your pet is provided on pages 56 and 57. In addition to that advice, it can be a case of trial and error to see whether your pet travels better in a safety harness, travel crate or loose in the back of the car, confined there with a dog grille.

As soon as you get your dog, accustom him to travelling in the car by taking him on short trips – around the block at first – and drive with care. Drivers, who have the steering wheel to hang on to, don't realize how uncomfortable sudden increases or decreases in speed, and cornering too sharply or quickly, can be for passengers (human as well as canine).

BELOW Ensuring that you transport your dog correctly and comfortably will help keep his travel stress to a minimum.

My dog loves chasing toys that
I throw for him, but how can I
teach him to retrieve them?

**As well as a chase toy, have a high-value
toy in your pocket.** Attach a long line to
your dog's collar and hold the end. Then:
1 Command your dog to sit by your side.
Throw the chase toy for him within the
range of the line and tell him to 'fetch'.
2 When he has picked up the toy, reel
him back in to you, all the while
encouraging him to 'fetch'.
3 When he reaches you, reward him
with praise or a treat and the high-value
toy. Repeat a couple of times and finish
on a positive note. Your dog has learned
that bringing the toy back to you will
earn him a reward.

4 In subsequent training sessions, once
your dog is repeatedly bringing back the
toy on command, let him off the long
line and try it. Hopefully, success should
now be yours.

I want to change my dog's
name. How do I do this?

**Choose a short name, as your dog will
recognize this more easily.** Use this
instead of his former name and he'll
soon understand (see page 58).

**BELOW Throwing a toy for your dog to retrieve is a
good way to ensure he gets adequate exercise, plus
it's an enjoyable activity for you both.**

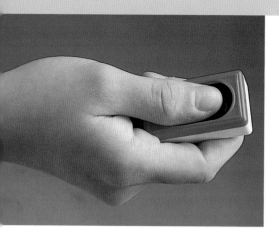

ABOVE **A clicker is suitable for training both puppies and adult dogs.**

RIGHT **Silent dog whistles (only dogs and other animals can hear them) come in all shapes and sizes to provide a range of pitches. You can even get a combined whistle and clicker.**

What is clicker training?

A clicker is a small hand-held tool that can be used to 'condition' good behaviour. It's simple but effective: just press and click.

The beauty of the clicker is that it is instantaneous: the moment the dog displays a desired behaviour, click, then reward him with a treat. The dog learns that the sound (which is reinforced by a treat) means a particular behaviour is good. Click, reward; no click, no reward. Being clever, dogs soon get the idea.

For example, to use the clicker to train your dog to sit:

1 Stand with your dog and wait until he sits.

2 As soon as he does, click and say 'sit'.

3 Reward him with a treat and praise him lavishly.

Can I use a dog whistle instead of spoken commands?

You can certainly use a whistle to signal commands. It would really help you to find a trainer who specializes in whistle training. Not only will they teach you how to use a whistle effectively, they will also be able to advise on which model would best suit you and your dog.

You need to work out a system for what certain calls and sequences of calls mean: for example, one short call for a recall, two for a stay and so on. Then teach your dog to respond to them in the same way as you would your voice. Just as with voice and/or hand signal training, a dog needs to be familiar with and understand certain calls and the expected response in order to comply appropriately. Stick to the system so as not to confuse your pet.

My dog is very badly behaved – would an electric shock or spiked collar be beneficial?

There are rare instances where the use of this equipment is appropriate, but only as a last resort. A trainer might use one in cases where there are no other viable options before a dog is put down for serious misbehaviour (for example, chasing livestock). Even then, such equipment should only be employed by trainers who are experienced and humane in their use.

In amateur hands (as is the case with the majority of dog owners), such equipment would be useless and cruel, since it is unlikely to be implemented correctly or appropriately.

Why does my dog misbehave?

This is the most common question trainers are asked. However, owners should also ask themselves whether their dog is misbehaving or in fact doing what he thinks is the right thing.

The main reason dogs 'misbehave' is because they have been forced into behaving that way by humans who have failed to train and stimulate them sufficiently. Does your dog receive enough physical and mental exercise? Do you send him conflicting signals – for example, letting him barge through doors before you one day and not the next? How often do you attend a training class to get expert advice? Some or all of these areas may need addressing in order for you to regain control.

It is important, however, to have your pet checked by a vet in case there is a physical ailment that is causing his problem behaviour.

My dog barks incessantly when in the car and sometimes vomits. Can I cure him of this?

Dogs generally behave like this because the sight of the world going by and the vehicle's motion makes them feel queasy. A warm, airless vehicle also causes stress. In addition, if you only ever take your dog in the car to visit the vet, he may associate the vehicle with an unpleasant experience, hence his agitation.

For advice on safe and comfortable travel, see page 149. If necessary, ask your vet (or a holistic vet) if there is any medication that could help settle your pet while travelling.

How can I stop my dog pestering me or other family members for attention?

The golden rule is only to give a dog attention when you decide to, not when he demands it. To cure your pet's attention-seeking behaviour:
1 Ignore him if he demands attention by jumping up at you or otherwise pestering you.
2 When he gets no reaction from you he will most likely stand still or sit down, and consider the situation.
3 Then he will lie down, considering what his next move should be.

4 Soon after he lies down, it is important that you reward this desired behaviour. This way, your pet will associate non-attention-seeking behaviour with a pleasant experience, and learn that leaping around trying to get attention brings no reward at all.

How can I accustom my dog to being inspected by myself or the vet?

Obedience training will enable you to have more control over your pet. This will also teach him that displaying a required behaviour earns a reward. You can use this principle to good effect when training him to be handled.

Teaching him to sit and stay in position will allow you to begin touching, stroking and inspecting the areas of his body he's most comfortable with. Give him lots of rewards every time he allows you to touch him. Progress slowly all over his body, leaving the most sensitive areas until last; after one positive touch, finish the session on that good note.

It will probably take many such sessions before your pet is at ease with you handling him all over. Consult your vet about giving rescue remedy to your pet before a visit, as this may help to calm and relax him.

BELOW LEFT Putting a reactive dog in a travel crate, along with his favourite blanket and toy plus an activity toy to help keep him occupied, and covering it with a blanket or sheet so that he cannot see the world passing, usually has a calming effect.

BELOW If a dog knows that hands bring rewards, he's less likely to react to them near his body and touching him.

How can I stop my dog biting when he is groomed?

This is a similar issue to handling (see page 153). However, if the problem is not in handling your dog, just in grooming, this could be because he finds grooming uncomfortable, so be gentle and make sure the tools you are using are appropriate for his skin/coat type. If his coat is badly matted, then teasing out knots can be extremely painful and it is kinder to clip off the coat.

If your dog is reacting to your professional groomer, it's worth taking him to someone else – a different approach and/or technique may just solve the problem.

BELOW Make your dog sit and wait for his food until you allow him to have it.

How can I stop my dog barging in front of me through doorways and up and down stairs?

The barging problem is a serious one, in that his behaviour is likely to cause an accident. It appears that your dog considers himself more important than you, so you will need to reduce his standing in the pecking order by being firm and not allowing him to have his own way. Enrol in a training class to get appropriate help before the problems develop into something worse.

In the short term, deal with the first problem by simply not allowing your pet to push past you through doorways; if he tries to, close the door in his face and keep repeating this until he desists. Prevent him from going up and down stairs by putting a stair gate across the bottom.

How can I stop my dog pulling on walks?

Don't pull back, as this will simply encourage the dog to pull more in an effort to escape discomfort. Nor should you yank on the leash, as this could damage your pet's neck.

Curing this problem is simple when you know how. See page 148 for how to implement heel training. Keep some smelly, tasty treats in a bumbag positioned on the side your dog is walking and give him one occasionally when he is walking in the correct position; this will help to keep him by your side.

Try using an anti-pull harness or a headcollar on your pet, as these can help alleviate pulling problems while trying to retrain.

ABOVE If your dog pulls, try the 'element of surprise' technique: simply stop dead and walk backwards. Then reposition your dog at heel and resume walking. The dog will learn that pulling is unrewarding and walking to heel is a more relaxed experience.

My dog doesn't do anything I tell him. How can I make him obey me?

An owner who is impatient and inconsistent is unlikely to have a rewarding relationship with a dog. You may be trying too much and too hard all at once or your training technique may leave a lot to be desired. Either way, the result is a confused and possibly frightened dog that has 'switched off' from you as a form of self-preservation.

To get on the right track towards a mutually fulfilling partnership with your pet, seek out the services of a good dog trainer. There is no substitute for on-the-spot expert advice and help in cases such as yours.

My dog gets bored with his toys, so I have to buy new ones to keep him interested while training. Is there any way around this?

You need to understand the value your dog places on a variety of different toys (see page 93). Swap your dog's toys around on a regular basis so that he doesn't have time to get bored with them; the selection you put away one week and bring out the next will seem new and exciting to him. You can keep this ploy going indefinitely.

My aged mother's small dog is fierce when he doesn't get his own way. She's reluctant to rehome him – what should I do?

The decision to rehome the dog rests with his owner, your mother. The only things you can do are:

● Point out the danger and your fears to your mother and suggest that she seeks home-training sessions to help her learn how to cope ably and safely with her pet. Offer to be there when the trainer visits.

● Suggest that she rehomes him for safety's sake, and offer to help her find a good home that she approves of for her pet.

ABOVE **Even the smallest, cutest dog needs to be trained and kept in its place, otherwise it will become the 'boss'.**

My dog doesn't come back when I call him. How do I solve this problem?

Take your dog out for exercise only when he's hungry, and wear a bumbag containing pieces of his favourite treats. Let him sniff them before you let him off the leash, and he won't go far away. Recall him, and reward him with a treat when he obeys; he'll soon realize that coming back to you on command is more rewarding than not doing so. You can use a high-value toy instead of treats if this motivates him better.

Never chase after your dog; he'll think this a great game and find it rewarding. Instead, walk away from him or hide; thinking he's being left, he'll most likely come after you. Do not scold him when he does eventually come back or he'll find recalling unrewarding.

Dogs who receive insufficient exercise and play are more likely not to recall.

How can I get my dog to walk by my side on the leash without stopping frequently to sniff things and/or urinate?

Your dog is more interested in sniffing to identify who else has been along that way, and then marking his own passage, than remaining at your side. You must be firmer with him and not allow him to 'train' you to stop whenever he feels like it; instead, insist he continues walking. Use a treat or a toy to keep his attention on you and to encourage him to keep up, or simply insist he remains at heel.

My trainer says I should smack my dog when he disobeys me, but I'm uncomfortable with this. What should I do?

Find a different trainer immediately – one who bases their training on reward rather than reprimand. Aggressive 'training' is non-positive: all it does is create a nervous and defensive dog, whose stress and bewilderment is likely to manifest in behaviour problems.

BELOW The bumbag technique is an effective way of keeping your dog by your side.

6

Health and wellbeing

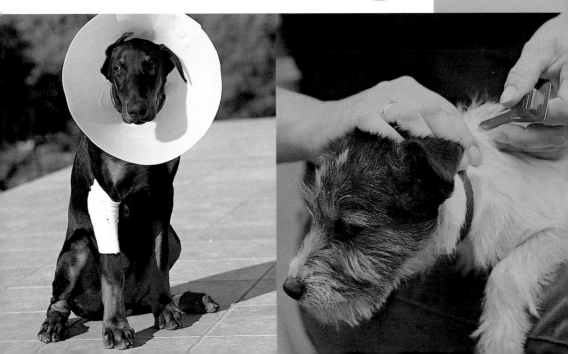

Can dogs sleep with their eyes open?

Yes they can, although the eyes are usually only partially open. This generally occurs briefly when the dog is dreaming.

If your dog's eyes are open all the time when he is sleeping, then this can be a problem as the eyes will dry out and there is a risk of foreign objects becoming lodged in them, neither of which is good for optical health. Dogs with bulging eyes are most prone to this condition; sometimes the eyes are so prominent that the lids cannot close all the way.

If your dog sleeps with his eyes open, have him checked by a vet; he may need surgery to correct lids that do not close fully.

Can dogs see in colour?

Research has proved that dogs can see in colour, but only to a limited extent. They have difficulty distinguishing the light colour spectrum between green, orange and red, but can distinguish blue, yellow, black and shades of grey. Green(y) colours are seen as 'white' and red(dish) colours as varying shades of yellow. The intensity of colours they can see is not as bright nor as clear as that which human eyesight can define.

Dogs can detect movement better than we can and see better in the dark.

Can dogs suffer ill-effects from passive smoking?

Yes, they can. Heavy air pollution, such as caused by smoking cigarettes in a small, enclosed environment like a house, can make existing respiratory conditions in dogs worse, as well as present the risk of lung cancer. At the very least, smoke

BELOW **A dog's colour vision compared to a human's.**

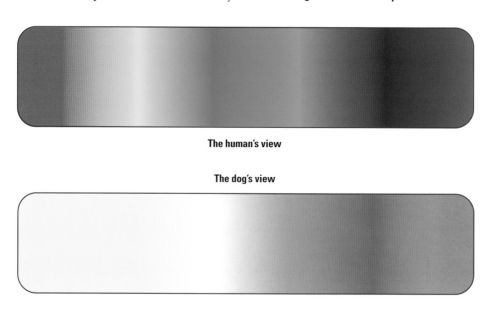

The human's view

The dog's view

ABOVE Dogs sleep for as much as 12 hours in a 24-hour period.

causes eye and nasal irritation, with flat-faced (brachycephalic) breeds being the most susceptible.

One study found that dogs in smoking households had a 60 per cent greater risk of lung cancer than those in non-smoking households. Research into the effects of passive smoking on dogs supports an association between environmental tobacco smoke and canine nasal cancer.

and exercise – the first to let their meal digest, the second to renew spent energy.

Dogs are adept at fitting in their daily amount of required sleep when their owners are also asleep; when their owners are awake and with them, the dog tends to be wide awake – and ready for any action that might be in the offing.

How much sleep do dogs need?

Dogs sleep for at least half their lives, which equates to around 12 hours in every 24. This is usually in periods of around 4–8 hours in any one undisturbed stretch. They tend to sleep as and when they feel the need, which is usually after meals

Can dogs swim?

All dogs can swim, although some are much better at it than others. This comes down to their body shape, stamina and overall physical ability. How much they enjoy it is another matter and depends

on their confidence in the water, although this can be bolstered by gradual acclimatization.

The risks for canine swimmers are the same as for humans: deep, cold water, fast-flowing currents and high banks that cannot be climbed easily all pose a danger.

How can I recognize if my dog is unwell?

Knowing your dog and what comprises his normal behaviour can, quite literally, be a lifesaver. Common symptoms of ill-health are indicated by:

- Obvious physical signs (wounds, bleeding, inability to move unaided)
- Digestive disturbances
- Coughing, sneezing or wheezing
- Eye/nasal discharge
- Pale/white gums
- Swollen abdomen
- Coat abnormalities

ABOVE Be aware that water pollution poses the same risks for dogs as it does for humans.

- Breathing difficulty
- Loss of appetite
- Hair loss
- Increased/decreased thirst
- Unusual eliminations (diarrhoea, blood in faeces or urine), constipation or urinating difficulty
- Odd behaviour (such as distress, depression or hyperactivity)
- Signs of pain (such as whimpering and limping)
- Fitting
- Stiff or unsteady gait
- Excessive salivation
- Apparent weight loss/gain
- Intolerance of exercise
- Lethargy
- Uncharacteristic aggression/nervousness
- The appearance of lumps

- Foreign objects lodged anywhere on the body
- Abnormal vital signs: normal temperature is 38.1–39.2°C (100.5–102.5°F); pulse 60–130 beats per minute (slower for large dogs); respiration 10–30 breaths per minute (less for large dogs). Normal pulse and respiration rates are naturally higher following exercise and in hot weather. The collective term for all three vital signs is TPR.

What should I do if my pet becomes ill?

Keep your dog quiet and warm and monitor his condition for 30 minutes or so. Note down his symptoms, when they started, how long they have been present and how his behaviour has been affected. Your vet will need to know all of these things in order to treat your pet quickly and effectively.

If the symptoms are severe and the dog is distressed, take him to the vet straight away – telephone first to warn them you are coming. The faster a poorly dog is seen by a vet the better, in order to effect a swift and complete recovery and minimize the distress to your pet (and you).

When is it necessary to take my dog to see a vet?

When any of the symptoms listed on page 162 are apparent. Sustained vomiting and/or diarrhoea in puppies should be treated straight away, as both cause dehydration in a couple of hours.

Veterinary attention should also be sought immediately if the dog has been involved in a road accident (see page 177), has suspected broken bones or has ingested a hazardous substance.

Other emergencies include:
- Burns and scalds
- Chemical burns
- Heatstroke
- Animal bites
- Insect stings and bites
- Convulsions
- Shock (following a trauma)
- Eye injuries
- Swallowing foreign objects
- Choking
- Electrocution
- Drowning
- Suspected poisoning
- Birthing difficulties.

ABOVE If you are concerned about your pet's health in any way, take him to the vet as soon as possible – better a false alarm than a tragedy.

How do I find a vet who is good at handling and treating dogs?

Veterinary surgeons are listed in local business telephone directories and also on the internet. Choose one who specializes in small animal care, specifically in dogs.

Word of mouth is a useful way of finding a good vet, as is contacting local breeders, dog training schools and/or dog rescue centres.

Does my dog need regular veterinary check-ups, and if so, how often?

Take your pet for a check-up at least once a year. To save on costs, combine the visit with his annual vaccination booster. Elderly dogs should be examined every 6 months.

It's worth keeping a diary of your dog's behaviour, health and vaccinations, as this is useful in helping your vet treat your pet appropriately and swiftly when the need arises.

Is veterinary help available if my dog becomes ill out of normal surgery hours?

All vets offer a 24-hour service for emergency treatment. If your regular vet is not available in an emergency, you will be advised by the practice of the nearest alternative vet who will be able to see your pet immediately.

Do you have to pay for veterinary treatment and how much does it cost?

You do have to pay for veterinary treatment. The cost varies depending on the surgery, its facilities and its location – city surgeries tend to be more expensive than those out of town due to higher overheads. It is always advisable to ring

BELOW Regular check-ups help identify health problems before they become serious.

round for quotes for non-emergency treatment, such as neutering and vaccinations, to ensure you get the best value for money.

It is also a good idea to take out pet insurance (see page 81) to cover veterinary costs should your dog fall ill or have an accident. Insurance does not cover cosmetic or routine treatment, such as vaccinations or neutering.

BELOW Canine surgery is usually expensive and insurance is a good idea.

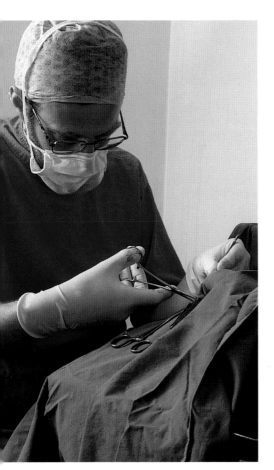

I'm on a low income – is any veterinary treatment available for free?

Some canine charity organizations offer free veterinary treatment for dogs whose owners are in financial difficulty. You will need to find out if there is a charity animal clinic in your area.

Some canine charities also offer reduced neutering costs to owners on low income or state benefits, including pensioners.

I'm not happy with the service I get from my vet. Do I need permission from them to change to another vet?

No, you don't. Simply go to a different vet and register as a new customer. Veterinary surgeries are private businesses, and if customers are not satisfied with the service they are free to go elsewhere.

How do I get a second opinion regarding the diagnosis of my dog's ailment?

If you would like a second veterinary opinion, you are entitled to ask for one. No one vet knows everything there is to know about their particular field of work.

Your vet will be able to arrange for a second opinion. They may even suggest consulting another expert in order to treat your dog most appropriately, especially if they do not have the specialized equipment or knowledge to deal with your pet's specific health problem.

Where can I learn how to treat my dog in an emergency, and to treat minor injuries/ailments?

A basic training in first aid will give you the confidence you need to deal with an emergency calmly and efficiently until an expert practitioner can take over. It will also provide you with the know-how to treat minor ailments, administer emergency first aid and resuscitation, and more importantly to recognize when veterinary attention is required. Many veterinary surgeries offer first-aid training, so contact those local to you.

What should I put in a canine first-aid kit?

Basic first-aid items can be bought from your vet, local pharmacy, and pet and veterinary supplies stores. In the canine first-aid kit listed opposite, essential items are marked with a star (*). Many items are the same as used for humans.

BELOW **Keep your first-aid kit stocked, replacing items as soon as they are used, and in a safe place that's easily accessible to you but not to your children or pets.**

FIRST-AID KIT

ITEM	USE
Surgical spirit	To remove ticks.
*Curved, round-ended scissors	To clip fur and trim dressings to size.
*Non-stick dressings	For cuts.
*Conforming ('sticky') bandage	To keep dressings in place.
Bandages	To keep dressings in place.
Syringe plunger	To administer liquid medicine.
*Cotton wool	To bathe eyes and nose, clean wounds and use as part of a dressing. Dampen before use to prevent strands breaking off and sticking to a wound.
Pencil torch and batteries	To inspect the mouth and ears.
Surgical gloves	To wear when treating wounds.
*Heavy-duty protective gloves	To wear when restraining a dog.
Sticky surgical plaster tape	To hold dressings in place.
Cotton buds	Can be dampened to remove grass seeds or other foreign objects from the eyes, and to clean wounds and apply ointments.
*Antihistamine	To ease insect stings and bites.
*Rectal thermometer	To ascertain temperature. You may prefer to use an aural thermometer, which is more expensive but can be easier to use.
*KY jelly or vaseline	To lubricate the thermometer before insertion.
Sterile eye wash, such as contact lens saline solution	For bathing eyes.
*Table salt	To make saline solution (2 teaspoons salt dissolved in 1 litre/2 pints warm water), with which to clean wounds and counter infection.

FIRST-AID KIT CONTINUED

ITEM	USE
*Antiseptic wound powder	For treating wounds and promoting healing.
Antiseptic lotion	For cleaning wounds – particularly animal bites.
Glucose powder	To make rehydrating fluid – mix 1 tablespoon glucose with 1 teaspoon table salt in 1 litre/ 2 pints warm water.
Space blanket or large sheet of plastic 'bubble wrap'	For wrapping around the dog to maintain body temperature in cases of shock and hypothermia.
Round-ended tweezers	To remove insect stings.
Elizabethan collar	To prevent the dog from interfering with dressings/sutures.
*Squares of clean cotton material (old linen or cotton bed sheets are ideal)	To place over wounds or stem blood flow.
Dog nail clippers	For clipping long nails (choose the guillotine variety).
*Absorbent paper (kitchen) roll	To wipe up any liquid mess.
Small stainless steel or plastic bowls	To contain saline or antiseptic solutions when bathing wounds.
Kaolin pectate	For treating diarrhoea. Obtain it from a vet and follow their dosage instructions.
*Muzzle	To place on an injured dog before you inspect him – if he's frightened and/or in pain, he may bite. A basket muzzle is best.
Styptic pencil	To stem the flow of capillary blood from minor cuts or bleeding claws and nails. Application stings, so muzzle the dog first.

What's the best way to treat cuts and grazes, and when do they warrant veterinary attention?

Most minor cuts and lacerations heal on their own fairly quickly. Treatment consists simply of keeping them clean with cotton wool dampened with saline solution. Initial bleeding, which may be profuse, helps to clean the wound of debris, reducing the risk of infection.

Veterinary attention should be sought immediately if:

- The wound is spouting bright red (arterial) blood in jets.
- There is a constant flow of dark red (venous) blood that refuses to cease.
- The wound is deep or serious enough to cause concern, as sutures may be required.
- Gunshot wounds are suspected.
- The skin has been punctured – these wounds appear tiny on the surface, but can be quite deep and are, therefore, particularly prone to becoming infected. Never attempt to remove a foreign object from such a wound, as this may aggravate the injury and/or allow large amounts of bleeding to occur (while it is in place, the object acts as a plug and may be preventing massive blood loss).
- The cut affects toes or a limb, as tendon damage may have occurred.

In the case of minor wounds, blood flow can be stemmed by gentle direct pressure using a dampened clean pad of cotton material, before cleaning. Where arterial or venous bleeding is present, apply indirect pressure (that is, not on the wound itself) to the appropriate artery or vein, if you can feel it under the skin, on the heart side of the wound; otherwise, press a cotton pad over the wound to help stem the flow of blood. Elevating the injury, if possible, will enable gravity to help reduce the blood flow.

If a dog requires surgery, is there any risk from anaesthetic?

There is always a risk, but these days modern anaesthetic drugs are much safer than they used to be. Incidences of side-effects and fatalities are, thankfully, rare. Dogs are also very carefully monitored while anaesthetized.

You can ask your vet to give your pet a thorough examination to check, as far as is possible, that being anaesthetized would present no problems. Ask them also to explain all the pros and cons, so that you are fully aware of all the facts.

Sometimes it is impossible to tell if a dog will have a bad reaction to anaesthetic, despite prior thorough checks. Unfortunately, in such cases, this is just extremely bad luck.

Do complementary therapies and treatments for dogs work?

Many owners and vets believe that they do. There are numerous tales and actual case histories recounting how natural medicine triumphed where conventional treatment failed.

There appears to be little scientific research to substantiate such claims where some therapies are concerned

LEFT **Complementary remedies and therapies can provide an effective alternative to conventional medicine. Chamomile has antiseptic and anti-inflammatory properties, making it useful for treating a range of ailments.**

I've just got an adult dog. Will he need vaccinating, or will he be immune to any diseases dogs can contract?

(such as spiritual healing and feng shui, for example), but these remedies have been used for thousands of years – and something that does not work is unlikely to have been persevered with for so long.

With most forms of complementary therapy, as long as they are applied with expertise and knowledge, the worst that can happen is that they have no effect. In many cases, they have been proved to bring about apparently miraculous cures.

Vets advise that dogs are vaccinated against those canine diseases that are highly infectious and/or life-threatening (see page 60). Unvaccinated dogs are at risk from these diseases.

If you want to show your dog, then most show rules state that vaccinations must be up to date.

How do I find a reputable vet who practises complementary therapies?

An increasing number of vets are turning to natural healing treatments. It is therefore relatively easy to find an experienced and genuine practitioner. Even if your own vet does not practise traditional medicine in the particular field in which you are interested, they may be able to refer you to a reputable practitioner who does.

If your vet will not refer you to a complementary practitioner, it may be advisable to take your business to another veterinary clinic that will.

My vet says my dog needs a booster vaccination every year. Doesn't a course of injections protect him for life?

A dog first receives his puppy vaccinations (or the initial course of vaccinations as an adult) against distemper (D), hepatitis (H), parvovirus (P), parainfluenza virus (Pi) and leptospirosis (L). He will then need a booster vaccination every year to maintain immunity.

The booster can comprise DHPPiL one year and PPiL the next, and so on, as the DH component lasts for approximately 2 years. Immunity can last for up to 6 months in some dogs after a booster is due, but for a shorter time in others; vets prefer to give boosters within 2 months of the last one lapsing.

ABOVE Having your dog vaccinated may not prevent him contracting an infectious disease, but it will lessen the effects and hasten recovery.

You can have your dog tested to check his antibody level (titre-testing), thereby ascertaining whether he needs vaccination boosters.

Are there side-effects from vaccinations which can make dogs ill?

Owners' concern about the risks associated with having dogs vaccinated have increased in recent years. There have been reports of dogs' immunity systems having suffered due to inoculation with vaccines.

There are instances where it may be inadvisable to vaccinate a dog:

● If he is ill, when he'll be unlikely to make a good immune response to the vaccine, and in fact it may worsen his condition.

● If he is receiving certain medications already that will affect his response to the vaccine. Some drugs suppress the immune system, and vaccination can exacerbate the condition for which the dog is being treated.

On balance, however, most vets advise that it is better to have healthy dogs vaccinated than run the risks of them not being protected. Controversy surrounds the use of the leptospirosis vaccine (which can be omitted from the routine vaccinations if the owner wishes), as it is this that is associated with an adverse reaction to vaccination.

What's the best way to keep my dog free from worms?

Complete wormers, which treat for both round- and tapeworms, are available from vets and are the most effective products to use (in terms of both cost and efficiency). Use when there is evidence that your dog has worms (see page 98).

Rather than give your dog an anthelmintic (wormer) when he may not actually need it, you can take a sample of your dog's faeces to your vet and ask them to do a faecal egg test to ascertain worm levels in your pet. Anthelmintics only kill worms at the time of worming; they do not provide immunity from worms.

You can give your dog natural worm repellents, but it would be advisable to consult a holistic vet who practises herbal medicine to find out which treatments would be suitable for your pet.

Medical research has shown that a moderate presence of parasitic worms in the digestive system can benefit humans with inflammatory bowel disease (IBD). It would be interesting if veterinary research were carried out along the same lines.

ABOVE Adding worming powder or tablets to appetizing food that your dog finds irresistible is often the simplest way to administer them.

What's the best way of keeping my dog and home flea-free?

Fleas bite and cause immense irritation (to both dogs and sensitive humans) and they also carry tapeworm. Fleas are also very difficult to get rid of if you do not keep on top of them, so ensure your pet remains flea-free by regularly using the most effective products (which are only available from your vet).

Flea eggs drop off dogs into carpets and soft furnishings, then hatch into adults which hop back onto the dog, beginning the cycle again. Regular vacuuming will help to remove flea eggs and larvae from carpets. Put a section of insecticidal flea collar in the vacuum bag (or bag-less cylinder) to kill any live fleas/larvae that are vacuumed up. Dispose of the bag/cylinder waste in the dustbin immediately afterwards.

Fleas love warm conditions, so a good summer is likely to see an abundance of them. If you have a real infestation, then you must have your home treated as well as your dog, and other pets, to get rid of them. Your vet will advise on the best course of treatment – routine and otherwise. When using flea products, follow the guidelines and instructions strictly, and never use more than one product at a time. Don't use canine flea products on other household pets as this can prove fatal to them.

Adding a teaspoon of brewers' yeast powder (available from health food shops) to your dog's food is said to help make your pet less palatable to fleas, as they don't like the taste of it.

How can I tell if my dog is underweight?

On a dog of ideal weight, you should be able to feel the ribs but not see them. You should be able to see just the outline of the last two ribs, but the rest should be covered by muscle and a thin layer of fat.

There is a good deal of difference between a dog being underweight, thin, very thin and emaciated.

BELOW **A spot-on flea treatment should only be administered at the back of the neck/between the shoulder blades, where the dog cannot lick it off.**

RIGHT **Health-wise, both mentally and physically, being too thin is as bad as being too fat.**

● In an underweight dog there will be some fat on the ribs, but he will have a visible waist and tuck-up. Being slightly underweight is preferable to being overweight.

● A thin dog's pin bones – the upper bony protuberance of the hip (pelvic) bones – will stick up above the muscle covering and surrounding them, and his backbone feels extremely bony and knobbly. He will have an obvious waist (area behind the rib cage, viewed from above) and visible tuck-up (area behind the rib cage and in front of the hindlegs, viewed from the side), and there is an absence of body fat.

● A very thin or emaciated dog will be skeletal, with an absence of muscle as well as body fat.

Some breeds, such as Greyhounds and Whippets, have no spare flesh covering their rib cage and have a natural tuck-up, so can look too thin to some people. However, provided they weigh the average for the breed, they are fine.

How can I tell if my dog is overweight?

If you cannot feel your dog's ribs, just a smooth outline, as you pass your hand over them, your dog is overweight. This is confirmed by a non-discernible waist and tuck-up (see page 175).

In cases of obesity, the ribs are completely covered by fat, and fatty deposits can be felt and seen at the base of the tail and over the spine. There will be no waist or tuck-up.

BELOW **Overweight dogs, like obese humans, can have shortened lives.**

My dog is a bit tubby. Should I put him on a diet?

Cut out snacks, increase his exercise and reduce his daily ration slightly. You could change the brand to one for less active dogs or one with a lower fat content.

If there is no discernible difference in a couple of weeks, take him to the vet for a check-up. Your vet will probably suggest a suitable diet and exercise regime for you to follow, along with regular weigh-ins to monitor your pet's progress.

Drastic diets do more harm than good – the key is to get your pet to his ideal weight slowly but surely.

RIGHT **Living with a flatulent dog is highly unpleasant, unless you have no sense of smell!**

How can I cure my dog's terrible flatulence problem?

Some dogs seem to be naturally 'windy'. Despite changing their diet and giving them charcoal biscuits (which can help to reduce gas production in the gut) nothing works, so unfortunately you may just have to learn to live with the problem.

Cereal-rich diets create flatulence in some dogs, while in others it's a high protein diet that's the culprit, so it is worth changing dog food brands and also trying natural diets (both home-made and commercial varieties) to see if this works.

Get your vet to check your pet in case an underlying health problem is causing excess gas. Causes of flatulence are summarized in the table below.

Should I take my dog to the vet if he vomits or has diarrhoea?

An occasional bout of vomiting or diarrhoea is usually nothing to worry about. Once the dog has rid his gut of whatever is causing the upset, he is fine again. However, with sustained vomiting and diarrhoea, especially when both occur at the same time, take your pet to the vet as he could quickly become dehydrated. He might also be suffering from a serious bacterial or viral infection.

DEALING WITH FLATULENCE

CAUSE OF FLATULENCE	WHAT TO DO
Unsuitable or poor-quality food that your dog is unable to digest properly	Change the brand of food; if it is of poor quality, try him on a better-quality diet.
Dog bolts his food, thereby swallowing air with it	Place large, smooth and clean stones in the food bowl, so he has to pick out the food; this will slow him down.
Feeding unsuitable table scraps	Stop feeding these scraps.
Serious digestive disorders	Consult a vet.

My dog is going deaf. How can I help him to cope?

The onset of deafness is usually due to old age, and nothing can be done to cure it. Train your dog to associate hand signals with spoken commands, while he can still hear them, so you will still be able to direct him when he loses all hearing. Teach him the visual commands for sit, stay, recall, stop and lie down.

My dog's teeth are very brown – are they rotten?

This staining is due to a build-up of two substances. The first is plaque (a sticky film on the teeth comprising a mixture of food deposits and saliva), the second calculus (a build-up of minerals, also known as tartar). You should take your pet to the vet to have his teeth checked. It is possible that they will only need a good clean, but on the other hand rotten teeth may need to be removed and infected gums treated.

Feeding mainly soft, tinned food may adversely affect the teeth, so provide crunchy food (kibble or biscuit-type feed) every mealtime to help clean your dog's teeth. Canine 'dental toys' may also help to clean teeth, as will raw meaty bones.

I discovered a small pale-coloured bug on my dog that was quite difficult to pull off. What was it?

This was a tick. Ticks are blood-sucking parasites that cause itchiness, infection and even paralysis in some countries. Ticks attach themselves very firmly to the

BELOW Where hard tartar invades gum space at the top of the teeth, pockets form that trap more food, leading to gum disease (gingivitis) and tooth decay.

BELOW If you live in an area where ticks are prevalent, check your dog for these parasites after exercise outside.

host by teeth and pulling them off often leaves their mouthparts imbedded in the skin, which then becomes infected.

Never remove a tick by force. Instead, use a special tick remover (available from vets and pet stores) to remove them safely. Alternatively, dab it with surgical spirit or flea spray that also kills ticks to make it release its grip. You can then pick off the tick with your fingers or tweezers.

What should I do if my dog is injured in a road accident?

If the dog is still in the road, stop the traffic so that you can safely recover him and/or administer the first aid that is appropriate (see page 166). Ask any bystanders or other motorists to call the police and request a vet. Approach the dog carefully and if it is safe to do so,

BELOW It's important to stay calm and clear-headed when dealing with a traffic accident involving a dog; do not put yourself at risk, as that won't help anyone.

examine him to assess injuries and, if necessary, whether you can move him without worsening his condition.

Speak softly to soothe him. Having administered appropriate first aid, keep the dog warm and calm until expert help arrives or someone can take him to a vet.

How can I treat a dog that has been electrocuted?

Switch off the power supply, then check that the dog is breathing. If not, begin artificial respiration. If it is not possible to switch off the power supply, do not approach the dog.

Electrocution will almost inevitably cause burns, which will need to be cooled with iced water for about 10 minutes to reduce the pain and severity. Cover the burn lightly with a cool, damp, clean and non-fluffy cloth (handkerchief or tea towel), wrap the dog in a space blanket (or equivalent) and take him to the vet for expert treatment.

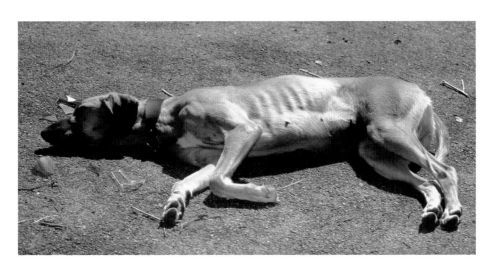

What should I do if my dog gets into difficulties in water?

Never go out of your depth in possibly dangerous water to rescue a dog. If you cannot get to him safely, call the rescue services. If you can get to the dog, follow this procedure:

1 Once you have pulled him from the water, hold him upside down (or lift up his back end if he's a large dog) to drain the water from his lungs.

2 Lay him flat and rub his body fairly vigorously to promote respiration.

3 If he is not breathing, commence artificial respiration (see page 166).

4 Summon veterinary help as soon as possible.

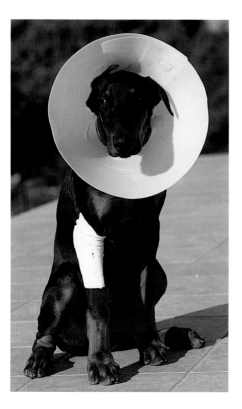

How can I stop my dog licking the medicated ointment off a sore on his paw?

An Elizabethan collar will be effective. It will also prevent him worrying at bandages, stitches and 'hot spots'. It comprises a wide plastic collar which fits around the dog's neck, preventing him from gaining access to his body with his mouth. You will have to take it off when he eats and drinks, if he has difficulty doing so.

Dogs don't like these collars at first, and will do their level best to get them off, so beware of him bumping into things in his efforts to do so. Distract him with an activity toy, a play session or a walk while he gets used to wearing it.

My dog keeps getting sore, wet patches on his legs and body – what can I do?

Such 'hot spots' are usually caused by eczema, resulting from a nervous reaction or an allergy. The latter might be in response to such things as too rich a diet, an ingredient in the diet, carpet freshener powder or washing powder residues in bedding. 'Hot spots' can also be due to flea bite dermatitis. Whatever the cause, the condition is exacerbated by the dog licking, biting and scratching at the affected area.

LEFT Elizabethan collars are used to prevent dogs from worrying sores and injuries, and prolonging the healing process.

Treatment comprises finding the cause, if possible, and eliminating it by trial and error. Your vet will supply an ointment to cool and soothe the area; udder cream designed for dairy cattle is also effective.

My dog gets itchy paws in summer. What is causing this and is there a cure?

There could be a number of causes. These include a grass pollen allergy, other allergy (see previous page), dust contamination, or an insect/parasite infestation obtained from grass. It could also be from walking on hot pavement/ground, or crop chemicals on fields.

After exercise, wash your dog's paws with salt water to remove anything that may be causing the irritation. If grass pollen could be the culprit, stay off grass while exercising. Try changing his diet to a more natural one (see pages 86 and 90).

Do dogs hurt each other when they fight? Should I separate fighting dogs?

Fights often look and sound more ferocious than they actually are. Rarely do dogs injure themselves, or each other; fights are usually over swiftly, with one conceding defeat quickly and becoming submissive, or turning tail and fleeing.

Never try to break up a fight with your hands as you may be bitten, nor try to break up the fight by shouting as this may well encourage the dogs. See below for how to separate fighting dogs safely.

Don't punish your pet for fighting, as some dogs associate their owners' aggression with the other dog, so the behaviour is perpetuated.

What's the safest way to break up a dog fight?

In cases where fights are sustained, try the short, sharp shock. Throwing a bucket of cold water over or turning a hose on the squabbling pair won't hurt them, but will cause them to stop fighting momentarily. In that moment you (and the other owner, if applicable) can get hold of the dogs to keep them apart, but only if it's safe to do so, and take them their separate ways quickly and quietly.

LEFT Anti-inflammatory and antihistamine injections or ointments can help to reduce pain and irritation in itchy paws.

My Jack Russell Terrier loves 'ratting'. Is it safe for him to do so?

There are some possible risks involved with canine pest control. These include abscesses caused by rat bites and leptospirosis, a potentially life-threatening bacterial infection. Incidences of the latter disease are, thankfully, rare.

Antibiotic treatment is usually successful if the disease is caught early enough. Vaccination will reduce the severity of the disease but not prevent infected dogs from becoming carriers.

BELOW **Ratting can prove risky for dogs.**

Is it true that grapes and chocolate can prove fatal to dogs?

Although many dogs enjoy eating chocolate if they have the opportunity to do so, quantities of it (particularly dark chocolate) can make them very ill – and even prove fatal. Don't give chocolate intended for human consumption as a treat; instead, give them chocolate drops specially formulated for canines. Some people give their dogs a grape (or raisin/sultana) as an occasional treat with the dog showing no ill effects, but there have been reported cases of grave illness and fatalities from dogs eating grapes and raisins.

Some dogs show no ill effects if they are given, or scavenge human foods, while others (especially those whose health is already compromised in some way) have a severe reaction to it and become very ill, or die.

BELOW **To be on the safe side, never feed your dog food intended for human consumption.**

Why does my dog appear to 'go off' his food in warm weather?

Dogs do not use up energy provided by food to stay warm in warm weather, so non-greedy dogs' appetites tend to reduce. Food quickly goes rancid in heat and becomes unappetizing, so uneaten food should be thrown away after 20 minutes (unless it's dry food, in which case give less). Wash the feed bowl after every meal to keep it fresh.

If not used quickly, open bags of dry food will become rancid in warm weather. Buy only enough food to last a week to ensure it stays fresh.

What should I do if I suspect my dog has eaten something poisonous?

Profuse salivation is the most obvious sign of poisoning, while sleepiness can indicate ingestion of rat poison. If you suspect your dog has ingested a poisonous substance, contact your vet

immediately and tell them what has happened – this allows the practice time to get information from the substance manufacturer while you are travelling with your dog to the surgery.

If you are instructed by the vet to make your dog vomit, place a couple of washing soda (sodium carbonate) crystals on the back of his tongue. Alternatively, use mustard or salt mixed with a little water.

What should I do if my dog swallows a foreign object?

If you know your dog has swallowed something potentially harmful, take him to the vet immediately. Choking, on the other hand, requires immediate action: trying to get the dog to a vet will waste time and may result in asphyxiation.

1 Check to see if anything is stuck in the dog's throat. Ask a helper to hold the mouth open while you remove any blockage. Don't push it further down his throat.

2 If the object is wedged in place, sit, lift the dog's hindlegs over your knees, then hold legs between knees. Place one hand on either side of the chest and squeeze using jerky movements, making the dog 'cough'. Squeeze 5–6 times and the dog should cough out the object.

3 Let your dog rest, and then take him for a veterinary check-up.

4 If the object does not come out, take the dog to the vet immediately.

LEFT **Make sure your pet does not have access to hazardous household substances.**

What should I do if my dog is bitten by another?

Clip away the hair from around the bite and clean the wound thoroughly with saline solution, followed by diluted antiseptic lotion. Dry the area, then apply a liberal dusting of antiseptic wound powder.

Repeat the treatment twice daily – it is important that the wound is kept clean, otherwise it may fester, become infected and result in an abscess. Dog bites almost always end up infected if they are not treated adequately.

What should I do if an insect stings my dog?

If the dog has been stung in the throat, seek veterinary attention immediately as swelling may block the airways and kill him. For stings elsewhere on the body:

ABOVE **Keep an eye on your dog in the garden during 'insect weather', to ensure he doesn't chase bees, wasps or other stinging insects.**

1 Clip the hair from around the affected area so that you can see it better.
2 Wash the area with saline solution (2 teaspoons salt in 1 litre/2 pints water).
3 Bees leave their sting in the victim, wasps do not. If you can, remove the sting with tweezers and then wipe the area with cotton wool dampened with surgical spirit.
4 To neutralize the effect of a wasp sting, wipe the area with vinegar; use bicarbonate of soda for bee stings.
5 Dry the area thoroughly but gently, and apply a wet compress to help reduce the irritation and swelling.
6 For other insect bites, clean and dry the area, then apply antihistamine spray or ointment to reduce itching.

Will neutering change my dog's temperament and character?

Usually, neutering has no adverse effect on temperament and character. Positive effects include helping to make hormone-related problems with difficult, excitable or aggressive dogs easier to deal with.

What are the disadvantages of not having dogs neutered?

Any disadvantages are minor (see pages 72–73) compared with those of leaving your pet entire. Entire males may become hyperactive and/or howl if they detect an in-season bitch, and also display marking behaviour in the house. They are also more likely to be antisocial to other males and more assertive towards their owners and other people, as well as being more at risk from testicular cancer and prostate problems.

The season of an entire bitch lasts for around 3 weeks, during which time she passes a small amount of blood-stained fluid from her vulva and attracts canine suitors – be prepared for Romeos lying in wait outside your house and on walks. In addition, entire bitches are at risk from cancerous mammary tumours and pyometra (a serious uterine infection).

RIGHT Bitches that are spayed before their first season tend to be more prone to urinary incontinence than those spayed after it.

Is it true that bitches can become incontinent after being neutered?

It is recognized in the veterinary profession that incidences of urinary incontinence are greater in spayed bitches than in unspayed. Female hormones play a part in the working of the bladder sphincter, so it is possible that the reduction of these after spaying is a contributory factor. However, incidences are rare, and those that do occur can usually be treated effectively with medication.

How soon can dogs resume normal life after being neutered?

Exercise on the leash for 2 weeks after the operation to prevent your dog leaping and running around, which could hinder the healing process. After this period, males can revert to normal life, but, as their surgery was more complex, bitches need another couple of weeks before strenuous exercise and jumping around can be resumed.

ABOVE Separation anxiety can lead to behaviours such as destructiveness and soiling in the house.

What is a monorchid dog and is this a problem?

A monorchid (or cryptorchid) is a dog in which one testicle has been retained in the abdomen or within the skin of the inguinal (groin) region. The dog can still father puppies, but may pass on the fault to his offspring so should not be used as a stud.

It is advisable to have the dog's undescended testicle removed surgically to prevent the risk of it becoming cancerous. It is usually advisable to have the other testicle removed at the same time.

My vet has diagnosed my dog with separation anxiety. What causes this?

Dogs dislike being left on their own as, being pack animals, it makes them feel vulnerable. Being alone affects some dogs more than others, especially those that have high dependency on their owners or who have previously been abandoned.

Owners should not encourage their dogs to become overdependent, as this will lead to problems. It is not fair on a dog to encourage him to be so highly dependent on you that he cannot let you out of his sight without feeling anxious.

I work full time – can I own a dog?

Dogs need plenty of care and enjoy lots of attention. For a dog to remain mentally and physically healthy, being at home alone all day while owners are at work is not the best environment.

Some people get around leaving their dog at home alone by employing a dog-sitter/walker, or a willing and able neighbour, to come in during the day to exercise and socialize with their pet. Other people drop their dog off at a boarding kennel on the way to work and pick him up again on the way home, which works fine if the dog is happy with this arrangement.

Another possibility is not to get a dog of your own, but to 'share' one with someone in your neighbourhood – perhaps someone who works at night, or is elderly and can no longer exercise their pet as much as they used to. Alternatively, you could offer to help out at a local dog centre during your free time.

BELOW RIGHT Do not force attention on a nervous dog – instead let him come to you.

BELOW Having someone look after your pet will keep him content while you are at work.

My dog was previously ill-treated and cowers at any sudden noise or movement. What should I do?

It's worth obtaining a dog-appeasing pheromone diffuser (available from vets). This releases a calming, reassuring scent into the air and will help to relax your dog, while you work on other elements.

Although you may feel sorry for the dog and that you have to make up for what has happened to him previously, do not be tempted to spoil him or you could be paving the way for other behavioural problems to develop later on. Treat him

as you would any other dog, but be careful not to raise your voice or make sudden movements towards him that could be misinterpreted as threatening. Do not put him in a position where he feels that he has to defend himself, or any of 'his' possessions.

Time, patience and kindness, combined with fair, clear directions, will help your dog regain his confidence and trust around humans, although bear in mind that some dogs never do feel completely at ease if they have been ill-treated in the past.

BELOW Provide your pet with activity toys to distract and occupy him during the time you are away from the house. Leaving a radio playing low can provide comfort, as the noise is familiar and therefore soothing and reassuring.

How can I keep my dog happy and amused while he's alone in the house?

You must gradually accustom your dog to being in the house alone. It is not fair to be with him all the time and then suddenly go off for the day without him, or he'll think he's been abandoned. Gradually increase the time for which you leave him alone, but it should never be for more than 4 or 5 hours (even less for a puppy).

When you return home, hang up your coat, put the kettle on or whatever, and only then turn your attention to your pet. This is to ensure that you do not elevate his position in the household beyond that of bottom of the pack.

Is it a good idea to take our dog on holiday with us (within our own country)?

Dogs are generally content to be where their owners are. They are happy to explore new places, so will enjoy going away on holiday together.

Take your dog's bed, toys, food, collar and leash, and also a first-aid kit. Find out where the nearest vet is in the area, just in case. Make sure your dog is wearing an ID tag bearing your holiday address and phone number as well as your permanent one, in case he gets lost. Have your dog ID microchipped or tattooed.

BELOW Always check out a boarding kennel yourself well before you need to leave your dog.

How do we find a boarding kennel to look after our dog while we are away?

Ask your dog trainer, other training class members, your local vet or your dog groomer if they can recommend an establishment. This is usually the best way of finding a suitable boarding kennel. Failing that, try checking in the pet sections of local newspaper advertisements and in the business telephone directory. Inspect the kennel yourself before you need to go away.

Kennels should be licensed by the appropriate local authority and have third-party and public liability insurance. Your pet's vaccinatons will need to be up to date.

What alternatives are there to leaving our dog in boarding kennels while we are away on holiday?

If you have a number of pets, employing a pet-sitter is a good and cost-effective option. Use a reputable agency that vets its staff carefully, and offers insurance in case of mishaps.

If leaving your dog in someone else's care, provide them with:

- Contact details for yourself and for your vet.
- Enough dog food (and a bit extra) for while you are away, and a list of how much food your dog is given and when.
- Medical details if your dog is receiving treatment.
- A list of any specific dos and don'ts regarding your pet's care and handling.
- Maps and duration times of safe, local walks.

How can we prepare our dog for being left in kennels for the first time?

Take your dog to the kennels to meet the staff and to play games with them there. Then take him again another day and leave him for an hour or so, with a toy and his bed for familiarity, before picking him up again, so that he learns you will come back for him. Progress to a day, and then an overnight stay.

My dog enjoys going on trips with me in the car – is it all right to leave him alone in it while I'm shopping?

There is a real risk of a dog getting heatstroke when in a car, either on a long journey or when left inside one. Inside a car, the ventilation is poor and the temperature rises to a dangerous level

LEFT **Never leave your dog unattended in a car on a warm day.**

quickly, even in the cooler sunshine of spring or autumn. If it's sunny, fix a sun screen to a window to provide some shade from the sun's full glare, and leave a window slightly open to maintain a flow of fresh air while you are driving.

I'd like to take my dog on holiday abroad with me – are there any restrictions?

These days, taking your dog abroad is much easier than it used to be due to the introduction of the Pet Travel Scheme (PETS). You will need to check both your home and destination country's rules and regulations regarding pet travel, as they do vary.

As PETS is a relatively new ruling, conditions change fairly frequently, so you need to find out from the relevant government department what documentation is required and which vaccinations, parasite treatment and ID are needed for your dog to leave and re-enter your country. One of the easiest ways to acquaint yourself with these details is to check your country's rules via the internet – simply key 'pet travel abroad' into a good search facility.

BELOW Don't forget to pack for your dog as well as for yourself when taking him on holiday with you.

7

Reproduction cycle

My 6-month-old cross-breed bitch has started to bleed from her 'bottom'. Why?

This is nothing to worry about. At this age, bleeding from the vulva indicates that your bitch has started her first season ('heat'), which will last for around 21 days. She will only allow herself to be mated 10–14 days into her oestrus, when the bloody discharge turns clear. This means that there are only a few days during the 21-day season when she is able to conceive.

Most bitches reach puberty at 6–14 months old.

How do male dogs know to hang around outside the house when my bitch is in season?

Once he is sexually mature, a male dog is always ready for mating. He will not normally take any notice of a bitch that is not in season, but will be attracted to her when her body releases the chemicals known as pheromones that indicate her sexual condition. This happens a few days before the bitch becomes sexually receptive.

How can I prevent my bitch having puppies?

An entire bitch can be extremely difficult to keep confined when in season. Her instincts drive her to do her level best to escape and find a mate, while suitors do their best to get to her.

The best solution is to have a bitch spayed to prevent her conceiving. If she is already in season, then ensure she does not come into contact with male dogs. This is easier said than done.

Can a bitch be spayed while she is in season?

When a bitch is in season, and for a while afterwards, her reproductive organs are engorged with blood, so there are greater risks involved in surgery. Some vets will spay an in-season bitch, while others prefer to wait for 3 months or so after a heat.

BELOW Male dogs can scent a bitch in season up to several miles away and, if they get the opportunity, will travel to find her and hang around awaiting their chance to mate. There may well be fights in the vicinity between rival males.

Should a bitch have at least one litter of puppies before being spayed?

This popular myth is based on human needs and emotional responses rather than scientific fact. There is no evidence to suggest that it is necessary to allow a bitch to have a litter in order for her to be a well-adjusted animal. If you want to raise a litter and are confident you can place the puppies in good homes, a bitch can be spayed after weaning to prevent further pregnancies.

ABOVE It may seem a nice idea to let your bitch have puppies before she's spayed, but bringing up puppies is time-consuming, expensive and messy.

Are there any contraceptives for dogs?

Hormone tablets can be given when the bitch is in season. These will prevent her conceiving if she is mated accidentally. Alternatively, a hormone injection can be given 1 month before the season is due. This prevents a bitch coming into season.

However, there are drawbacks to prolonged birth-control treatment. Vets do not like to prescribe it, since it can have serious side-effects, such as the development of pyometra (a life-threatening uterine infection), nor is it 100 per cent effective.

Chemical castration (comprising an anti-testosterone drug) is available for males, but is not always effective and dogs can – and will – still mate bitches.

Surgical neutering remains the safest and most effective option.

BELOW A simple vaginal smear, taken up to 24 hours after an alleged accidental mating, will confirm whether or not a bitch requires drugs designed to prevent pregnancy. This is the safer option, rather than administering potentially risky medication that may be unnecessary.

My bitch escaped while in season and may have been mated. What should I do?

There are more efficient 'morning-after' drugs available for dogs now than there used to be. The traditional treatment was to inject the bitch with a large dose of female hormone (oestrogen) within 36–48 hours of an accidental mating (misalliance), to prevent conception. However, this treatment was not 100 per cent effective, and could induce pyometra and blood/bone marrow disorders.

Safer alternatives can now be administered by a vet, comprising either an injection of female hormone between the third and fifth day post-mating to prevent conception, or two injections 24 hours apart up to day 45 of the pregnancy to induce abortion.

How old must a bitch be before she can have puppies?

Often bitches come into season at 6 months, but are not physically or mentally mature enough to cope with puppies. If mated at this tender age, pregnancy could stunt a bitch's growth and spoil her as a future breeding bitch, so it is better to wait for her second season before breeding from her. Some bitches have their first season at 9 months, and the same rule applies.

It is usually safe to mate a bitch if her first season occurs at 12 months, but it is preferable to wait until she is 18 months old before breeding from her.

At what age can a male dog sire puppies?

Male dogs are able to sire puppies from around 9 months of age. If a dog is to be used as a stud, his first mating should be with an experienced brood bitch, to help ensure all goes smoothly and that he is not injured.

Is it possible for dogs to be infertile?

Both male and female dogs can fail to produce puppies, for a variety of reasons:

- Sexual immaturity
- Over- or underweight
- Malformed (or non-existent) reproductive organs
- Abnormal oestrus cycles in females
- Low sperm count or poor-quality sperm in males
- Mating at the wrong time
- Nutritional deficiencies
- Lack of opportunity to mate
- Sterility due to medication, now or in the past
- Disease.

My 2-year-old bitch has been mated twice, but failed to conceive. Why?

One of the most common reasons for a bitch failing to conceive is her being mated either before or after ovulation. It is best to mate the bitch several times over the few days during which she will accept the male dog's attentions.

ABOVE **Some bitches have their first season as young as 4 months old.**

ABOVE **There are only a few days in a bitch's season when she is able to conceive from a mating.**

Other reasons include infection in earlier life, running a high temperature at the time of mating, or a hormonal imbalance. In some cases, evidence of pregnancy is seen but does not progress due to reabsorption or abortion of the embryos for some reason.

If the bitch has been mated to the same dog who is unproven as a stud, then the fertility problem could lie with him. Alternatively, the bitch may not yet be mature enough to conceive, although this is unlikely.

Can dogs get sexually transmitted (venereal) diseases?

Yes they can, though it is uncommon. Venereal diseases that affect dogs are the canine herpes virus (CHV), canine brucellosis and venereal granulomas (tumours).

I'd like my bitch to have puppies. Is this a good idea?

Before mating your bitch, ask yourself the questions below. Only go ahead if you can honestly answer 'yes' to all of them. Bear in mind that it's not advisable to breed two fighting breeds together.

● Is your bitch suitable to breed from? See opposite page.
● Can you afford the time, anxiety, mess, inconvenience, and the expense of stud and vet fees?
● Will you improve the breed in terms of conformation and temperament?

● Have you researched the stud dog's pedigree and ensured his line is free from problems?
● Do you have suitable whelping (birthing) accommodation?
● Can you cope with possible tragedies, such as the bitch losing the puppies, the bitch dying, or the puppies dying during/after birth or through illness later on?
● Will you be able to find suitable, permanent homes for the puppies?

BELOW Hip X-rays in breeds that are prone to hip dysplasia will show whether there is a fault in the hip joints.

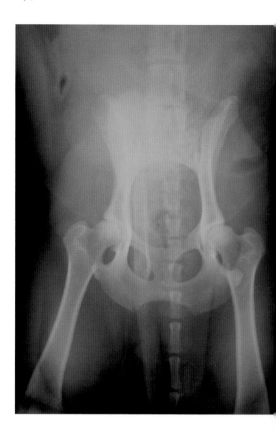

What is 'health screening'?

Many pedigree breeds are subject to certain hereditary defects. These include hip dysplasia, heart and/or eye defects, luxating (dislocating) patella and deafness. Responsible breeders screen their stock to see if they meet the approved health standard, as laid down by the appropriate canine governing body. In this way, their progeny will not carry the fault.

Your vet will advise on the appropriate tests, as will reputable breed clubs.

How do I know if my bitch is suitable to breed from?

Only breed from a bitch if she is healthy, fit, mature enough and good-tempered. If a pedigree, she should be a good example of the breed and come from a blood line free from hereditary defects.

ABOVE It is not a good idea to breed from a nervous or aggressive bitch, as her puppies are likely to develop the same traits.

If you join a breed club, other breeders are generally happy to discuss and assess your bitch.

How do I find a suitable sire to mate with my bitch?

Contact other breeders of the same breed (if applicable), as they may have studs or know people who do. Visit potential stud dogs so that you can assess their standard and temperament, and also the conditions in which they are kept. Steer clear of dirty, unkempt establishments, as this is usually an indication that the dogs' care and welfare is not all it should be.

Health Screening • Suitability • Studs **197**

Check the pedigrees of potential studs to ensure the lines are not too closely linked to those of your bitch, and do some research to ascertain if they are free from hereditary defects. Pedigrees will also indicate show successes in the stud's lineage. You may have to travel quite a distance to find the ideal stud, so be prepared for this.

Do all of this well before your bitch is due to come into season, so that you have a suitable mate lined up for her when she does.

Do you have to pay for the services of a stud dog?

You will usually have to pay a stud fee. The cost of this depends on how experienced the stud is, and if he is a champion and therefore much sought after by owners of bitches.

Sometimes, other arrangements can be made that suit both parties. For example, the stud's owner will agree to having the pick of the litter, taking one or two puppies rather than a fee at mating.

Always get the breeding terms in writing beforehand, so that you know exactly where you stand. Some breeders will allow you to have another service free if the first does not result in a pregnancy, but this is not a standard practice, especially if the stud is proven.

If you wish to register the puppies, contact the appropriate kennel club to see what documentation you will need in order to do so. Ask if you will need to get a stud certificate to prove that the mating took place.

I would like my handsome 3-year-old pedigree dog to be a stud. How do I go about this?

Your dog's potential as a stud could be put to the test by showing him. Showing results will confirm whether or not he is a good example of the breed.

Another way of finding out is to consult breeders of the same breed. If they judge your dog has the necessary attributes (good conformation, suitable temperament and pedigree free from hereditary defects), one of them may allow you to try him on one of their experienced bitches to confirm that he's fertile and to see what progeny he sires.

If you use your pet as a stud, bear in mind that he will need plenty of bitches to serve per year (which isn't a problem for quality studs as they are in high demand), otherwise he could very well become frustrated, which may lead to behaviour problems. A prospective stud learns that sexual play and behaviour is acceptable from puberty, whereas a pet dog usually learns the opposite through being admonished every time he attempts to mount someone's bitch (or leg!).

You will need to teach your potential stud to accept being handled while he's mating. This is so that, if necessary, you can help mating be achieved or prevent either dog hurting itself during intercourse.

Studs are at risk from sexually transmitted diseases (see page 196), so potential mates should have a current clean bill of health, and you should also have your dog tested regularly to ensure he's healthy.

I'd like my Bulldog bitch to have puppies, but have heard it can be risky for this breed. Is this so?

Unfortunately, yes. You need to be very dedicated to embark on Bulldog breeding and well prepared for all the risks involved to both mother and puppies, plus the expense and time involved.

BELOW A good way of deciding whether you want your dog to be a stud is to join a relevant breed club and learn all about stud work. This will tell you whether or not it is for you.

The problem is that Bulldogs have huge heads in relation to their bodies, so giving birth naturally is often impossible for this breed as the puppies' heads won't fit through the mother's birth canal. Pregnant bitches usually have to have a Caesarean section to help ensure both they and their puppies survive, with the surgery and bitch's aftercare resulting in great expense to the owner. Some bitches are so traumatized by surgery and the pain afterwards, that they refuse to have anything to do with the puppies. This means that the pups have to be reared by hand, unless a foster bitch can be found.

ABOVE **A tie can last from a few minutes up to half an hour or so.**

Another complication is that, being flat-faced (brachycephalic), Bulldogs suffer respiratory problems and administering anaesthetic to pregnant bitches in order to perform a Caesarean section carries its own risks, to both the expectant mother and the foetus(es).

Why do some mating dogs become stuck together, tail to tail? Should they be separated?

This is quite normal and is called a 'tie'. It happens after the male has mounted and penetrated the bitch and her vaginal muscles tighten around his penis, holding him fast until the muscles relax.

The tie prevents sperm-bearing fluid escaping during its transition from dog to bitch and, although it is not necessary for a successful mating, it does improve the chances of conception.

Do not attempt to separate the dogs or you will cause them great pain and possible injury. Separation will happen naturally.

How can I tell if my bitch is pregnant?

There are several different ways, depending on timing:

- Around 21 days after mating, your vet or an experienced breeder will be able to feel tiny 'lumps' in the abdomen, indicating foetuses. After 35 days these lumps will be softer and more difficult to feel, due to the protective (amniotic) fluid around them.

WHAT IS THE GREATEST NUMBER OF PUPPIES IN A LITTER?

According to the *Guinness Book of World Records*, three large-breed bitches hold the record for the largest number of puppies in one litter – 23 – although not all the puppies in each litter survived.

The American Foxhound had her puppies on 19 June 1944, the Great Dane delivered hers in June 1987, and the St Bernard had her litter in February 1995.

- By the fifth week, the bitch's teats will be larger and pinker, and her abdomen will be enlarged.
- By the sixth or seventh week, the mammary (milk) glands enlarge, and milk may be present (or overflowing).

How many puppies does a bitch have?

The number of puppies in a litter is normally regulated by the size of the bitch. A small bitch can have up to 5 puppies, a medium-sized bitch up to 8 and a large bitch up to 12 or more. Generally, nature dictates that a bitch will have no more puppies than the number of functional nipples she has.

Where abnormally large litters have been reported, some may have to be either fostered or hand-fed.

ABOVE **Larger breeds tend to have larger litters of puppies.**

ABOVE TOP **Ultrasound can safely be used to detect pregnancy at around 24–30 days after mating, although experienced users can detect foetal life at 15–17 days. Blood tests and X-rays can also be employed to confirm pregnancy.**

How long does a canine pregnancy last?

The canine gestation period (pregnancy) normally lasts for 9 weeks (63 days). Sometimes the puppies are born a couple of days before or after the due date.

Puppies who are premature by more than a week have a greatly reduced chance of survival, while those who are overdue are better equipped for life but their size can present birthing difficulties.

BELOW Just like pregnant women, heavily in-pup bitches should be encouraged to take things easy as the birth date approaches.

Does my bitch need any special care while she is pregnant?

There are several areas you need to attend to:
● Keep your bitch free from parasites – your vet will advise on the safest and most suitable treatment.
● Keep her coat well groomed, removing dead hair.
● If she is unable to clean herself adequately due to carrying a large litter, then sponge her anal area after toileting.
● A pregnant bitch's exercise routine need not change, but as she becomes heavier she will naturally slow down.

What should I feed my pregnant bitch?

An expectant mother needs extra food to maintain condition and provide for the puppies growing inside her. However, you must take care not to overfeed her: she should be fit, not fat. The easiest option is to feed your pet commercial protein-rich diet formulated for pregnant bitches; provide as much fresh water as she wants.

In the first 3 weeks of pregnancy, keep the diet as normal; thereafter the puppies grow fast, so step up your pet's protein-rich food intake. As the bitch becomes heavier, it is better to split her daily food allowance into smaller meals.

If she becomes constipated, substitute one of her daily meals with sardines or pilchards, as the oil content should aid defecation.

What ailments should I look out for during my bitch's pregnancy?

Healthy bitches usually cope very well with pregnancy. However, if your pet shows signs of being unwell then take her to the vet quickly.

Possible problems include miscarrying the pups, either because the foetuses are not healthy, or due to illness or infection.

RIGHT **Heavily pregnant bitches may need help in grooming, as well as cleaning under their tail. Trim excess hair around the nipples in bitches with long coats so that the puppies can feed easily.**

BELOW **The occasional raw or boiled egg (one or two a week, depending on the bitch's size) provides a good source of protein for pregnant bitches, but be aware that raw eggs pose a similar risk to dogs as they do to humans.**

Can my pregnant bitch be bathed and clipped?

Yes, but if she struggles while wet bathing it is safer to use a dry shampoo. When wet bathing, ensure she has a non-slip surface to stand on, you have someone to hold and steady her, and that you dry her properly afterwards.

Towards the end of pregnancy, trim excess hair from her trousers, skirt (stomach) and very carefully from around the teats. The first two will aid hygiene and ease of delivery, and the last will make it easy for the puppies to find the nipples and to suckle.

Is it safe to treat my pregnant bitch for fleas and worms?

Do not use over-the-counter remedies for internal and external parasites in pregnant bitches. Instead consult a vet, who will advise on and prescribe suitable treatments that are safe to use. These prove more cost-effective in the long run.

Ideally, bitches should be wormed before being mated, but if this was not done then do it 3 weeks after mating. If neither of these options is taken, then it's best to wait until after your bitch has whelped (given birth).

Why did my bitch abort her puppies?

This rarely happens, but if something is abnormal with the pregnancy the bitch will reabsorb or abort the whelps (unborn pups). This can be caused by:
- Hormonal irregularity
- Uterine infection
- Venereal disease
- Internal parasite infestation.

It can also be due to the bitch absorbing or ingesting a substance that is harmful to the foetuses – which is why it is wise to consult your vet regarding worming and de-fleaing products for pregnant bitches.

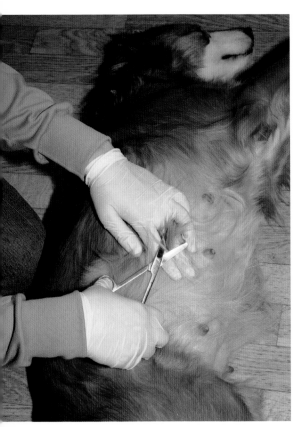

LEFT Take great care when trimming hair around the bitch's nipples. This procedure only needs to be done if she has a lot of fur on her belly, which can make it difficult for pups to feed.

Do bitches need any veterinary help when giving birth?

The majority of bitches instinctively cope very well themselves with giving birth. This applies even to first-time mothers (maidens), so it is rarely necessary to call for veterinary intervention. If you are worried about anything, then contact your vet who will advise you on what to do.

BELOW Scratching around in her bed or the place that she has chosen to have her pups is normal behaviour for a bitch in the first stage of labour.

How will I know when my pet will have her puppies?

As the birth becomes imminent, your bitch will do some or all of the following activities, as she enters the first stage of labour:

- Become restless
- Refuse food
- Tear up her bedding
- Look anxious and uncomfortable
- Whimper
- Pant.

There may also be a clear, mucus-like discharge from her vulva and she'll spend lots of time cleaning herself.

Do I need to stay with my pet while she has her puppies?

It is wise to do so, especially with maiden bitches, to observe that all is going well. You will also be able to lend a hand if needed or contact the vet should anything go wrong. Warn your vet well in advance of your pet's expected due date in case you need his help out of surgery hours.

How long does it take for a bitch to give birth?

There are three stages to labour. The first stage (see page 205) can take up to 24 hours. The second stage occurs when contractions start; after the first puppy is born, the rest usually follow at 10- to 60-minute intervals. The third stage is when all the puppies have been delivered, along with their afterbirths (one for each puppy).

How will I know if things are going wrong during the birth?

If the bitch has been straining to give birth for longer than an hour without producing any pups, consult your vet immediately. It is likely that a puppy is stuck in the birth canal.

BELOW Most births occur at night. Sometimes the warning signs of imminent labour are so slight that owners fail to recognize them and find the bitch with her litter in the morning.

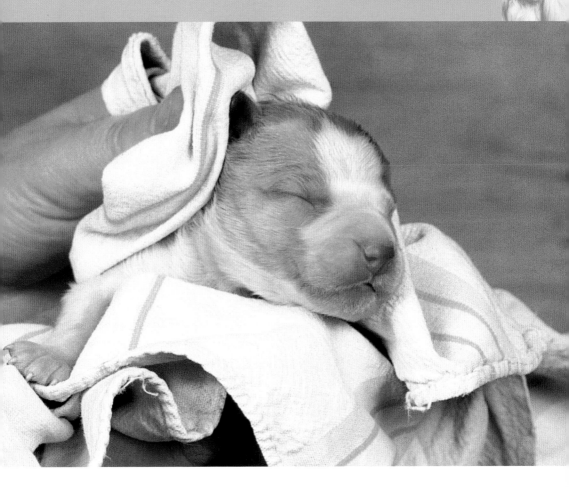

ABOVE **If the bitch is slow to wash her babies, then dry them gently with a towel.**

Breech births (where the puppy arrives hindquarters rather than head first) can present problems and, again, veterinary help may be required. Similarly, abnormal presentations (where, for example, the puppy is positioned sideways in the birth canal) will need expert assistance, though this is rare.

If the bitch shows signs of distress or exhaustion during labour, it is sensible to seek veterinary assistance as soon as possible.

What should I do after the birth?

The number of afterbirths (placentas) expelled should correspond with the number of puppies born. If one is retained it can cause a fatal infection. If your bitch appears to become off-colour within a few days of whelping, then seek immediate veterinary assistance.

It is doubtful that the bitch will accept food until all the pups have been born, but water (with glucose added for energy) should be available to her. The bitch will bite the umbilical cord to separate each puppy from its placenta (which she will eat), and then clean the baby.

Once delivery is complete, the bitch will appreciate a light meal of egg and milk, or cereal and meat broth, and may want to go outside to toilet (at which point you can remove soiled bedding and replace it with fresh); then leave her alone to rest quietly with her puppies. Check that they are all feeding.

Are there any ill-effects my bitch could suffer after giving birth?

Problems that can arise following birth include:

● Uterine infection, indicated by fever, vomiting, lack of appetite, and a dark-coloured, often smelly, vaginal discharge.

● Prolapsed uterus – indicated by a swollen red mass appearing out of the vulva.

Consult your vet immediately if any of these instances occur.

Where is the best place for my pet to have her puppies?

This depends on where your bitch is used to being kept. If she normally lives outside, then she'll probably be most at home in her usual housing.

BELOW Ensure outdoor whelping and puppy-rearing facilities are dry and warm enough – extra insulation will be required in cold, damp weather.

ABOVE Orphaned puppies need to be bottle-fed every 2 hours for the first week. Human baby teats are usually too large for puppies' mouths, so puppy teats are used. These are available to buy from pet shops and veterinary clinics.

If your bitch is house-kept, then she should have her puppies inside.

Should the bitch have her puppies in a bed or on a blanket on the floor?

A suitable whelping box of the appropriate size should be provided for the birth and placed in a quiet part of the house. You can buy these from pet stores, or alternatively make one yourself – a sturdy cardboard box often fits the bill admirably.

Line the box with a good thickness of newspapers on the bottom, covered with veterinary bedding or a clean cotton sheet to help prevent the bitch and her babies being contaminated with newsprint, and also to provide comfort and warmth. If you can get hold of unprinted newspaper, then this would be preferable.

A bed with sides makes the mother feel more secure, prevents the puppies from rolling out and protects the newborns from draughts.

How should I care for the puppies if the bitch dies after giving birth, or fails to produce enough milk?

If this happens, you will have to feed the puppies yourself. You will need to use a special puppy milk formula (not cow's milk), fed in a puppy feeding bottle or dropper. This milk is available from good pet stores and veterinary surgeries. Consult your veterinary surgery for advice on feeding the puppies – they may even know of a foster mother.

After feeding, clean the puppies by wiping their faces and paws with water-dampened cotton wool. Stimulate them to pass urine and faeces by gently wiping their tummies and anal areas with damp cotton wool (the bitch normally does this: without stimulation, the puppies cannot eliminate waste products from their bodies and will die). Then dry those areas.

BELOW Because their stronger, bigger siblings will push them out of the way, you need to keep a close eye on the smallest puppies in a litter to ensure they get their fair share of milk and warmth in order to thrive.

You will need to use a heat lamp, hung high above the bed, or a well-padded hot water bottle to replace the bitch's body heat in the nest – a temperature of 26°C (80°F) is required.

Hand-reared puppies usually wean early (see previous page).

What should I do if any of the newborn puppies appear unwell?

It is imperative that puppies who appear unwell receive veterinary attention quickly. This will give them the best possible chance of survival.

RIGHT It is wise not to handle newborn pups too much as this can unsettle the mother. In some cases, a nervous mother will eat her own babies in a desperate effort to 'protect' them.

In warm weather, fleas can be a real problem as they soon cause anaemia in young puppies, and it is essential that veterinary advice is sought on how to treat them.

What is meant by the term 'runt'?

The term 'runt' is often used to describe the smallest pup in a litter. This can be because it didn't receive as much nutrition in the womb as its siblings, or because it is unhealthy. In the former case, the puppy should soon increase in size provided it receives enough food from its mother, and then when weaning starts. However, although healthy, some runts simply don't grow as big as their littermates.

If the runt is unhealthy, it may die soon after birth or before weaning. If it doesn't die, then it may always be susceptible to illness.

Why won't my bitch let me near her newborn puppies?

New mothers are instinctively protective of their offspring – some more than others. They can guard them fiercely, especially if they judge that a person's presence could be a threat to the babies.

Your pet is probably quite capable of looking after her puppies herself and doesn't want to share them with anybody – even you. After about a week she will soften when the novelty wears off, she is confident that there is no threat to them, and she needs a break from them from time to time.

How soon after birth can I handle the puppies?

As soon as the bitch will let you, but don't try to take them away from her. Pet her first, to let her know your intentions are good, and then pet the puppies if she will allow you to do so. Speak to her softly and soothingly – and remember that they are her babies, not yours.

ABOVE **An adequately fed bitch will provide enough milk for her babies.**

What do puppies eat?

For the first 3 weeks they survive and thrive on their mother's milk alone. If the litter is a large one, supplementary feeding as soon as the puppies will accept it will take the strain off the bitch and ensure the babies receive enough nutrition (see page 209).

How do you keep puppies and their bed clean?

The bitch will keep the puppies clean, and also clear up their urine and faeces from the bed until they start to be weaned. Change the bedding every other day to minimize the risk of infections, and to keep both bitch and puppies clean and as sweet-smelling as possible.

Once the puppies are on the move you can wash their feet and bottoms as necessary, but make sure you dry these areas thoroughly afterwards.

My bitch's puppies died in the week following their birth. Why?

If the bitch is not very maternal, she may not have been stimulating them to toilet effectively. If this was the case, the build-up of waste products in their bodies will have caused the puppies to stop feeding and die. Other possible reasons include:

- Insufficient nutrition
- Cold
- The bitch lying on them
- Infection
- Genetic ailment.

Sadly, my bitch's puppies died and she seems really upset. What should I do?

Sometimes, for various reasons, puppies do not survive. If the bereaved bitch appears distressed, contact your vet for advice as she may require medication to suppress her milk and help prevent potential mastitis. Her loss may have a happy ending if the vet knows of orphaned puppies needing a foster mum.

BELOW If her puppies die, distract your pet by playing with her and taking her for favourite walks; you'll find that she will soon get over her bereavement.

My bitch had her pups a week ago, but there is still a discharge from her vulva. Is something wrong?

It is normal for a blood-stained discharge to pass from your bitch's vulva for a week or so after she's given birth. This will gradually become clearer, until it stops altogether.

However, if the discharge is foul-smelling and accompanied by signs of vomiting, loss of appetite, dullness, fever and distress, then the bitch is likely to have a uterine infection, probably caused by the retention of an afterbirth. Such symptoms need immediate veterinary attention.

My bitch's teats are red, swollen and feel hot. What's wrong with them?

This can happen when there is an excess of milk or the puppies are not sucking on all her teats. Massage the teats and, if your pet will allow it, draw off some milk to ease the pressure. Try putting the puppies on the teats they have been ignoring, to encourage them to suck from them as well as the others.

Hard, hot teats, which may produce bloodstained or abnormal-looking milk, can also be a sign of mastitis, a bacterial infection. In this case, the bitch will go off her food, appear distressed and may vomit. Seek immediate veterinary advice.

My pet seems permanently hungry following the birth of her puppies. Should I give her more food?

While she is lactating, a bitch will eat and drink more than normal to maintain a plentiful milk supply. Increase her food intake to around three times her usual amount, split into three or four meals a day.

Her diet needs to be rich in calcium, protein, vitamins and minerals to sustain her body's needs, plus she needs a constant and plentiful supply of fresh, clean water to encourage good, nutritious milk production.

Make sure that your bitch cannot get access to the kitchen waste bin, or other food sources that could prove harmful to her and/or the puppies.

My bitch's puppies are 2 weeks old and feeding well, but are scratching her teats raw and she seems sore. What should I do?

The puppies' nails should be cut (only the curved tips) once a week until they are weaned, to prevent them scratching their mother. A cooling and soothing healing cream that is non-toxic to both her and the puppies can be used on the teats between feeds – ask your vet for advice on a suitable product to use.

BELOW Feeding puppies takes a lot out of a bitch, so make sure she receives enough suitable food to cope with the demands on her body.

Now that my puppies are moving around, how can I confine them to reduce the mess they make?

A large puppy pen is a good investment. You can put the pups in it when they are in an exploring and playing mood, both to reduce mess around the house and to provide the mother with periods of much-needed rest.

Place the pen on top of a waterproof cover to protect the flooring (an extra square of vinyl floor covering is ideal) and lay several layers of newspapers over this – these can be changed as soon as they are soiled.

Encourage the puppies to soil in one designated place in the pen, by placing a small amount of their faeces in a low-sided large cat-litter tray (or an old baking tray) containing newspaper. Sometimes this works, sometimes it doesn't. If it does, it can make house-training easier.

My bitch has started to vomit her food back near her puppies. Why?

She is trying to wean her puppies. This always happens in the wild, and often with good maternal domestic bitches too. As the food is partly digested it is easier for the puppies to digest, but as you wean them she will stop doing this.

LEFT Feed puppies from shallow bowls so that they can get at the food easily.

My bitch seems to play really roughly with her puppies and makes them squeal. Should I stop her?

Your bitch is teaching the youngsters to fend for themselves and the rudiments of the pecking order. Don't intervene unless she really is hurting them.

From 3 weeks onwards, the puppies will start to play-fight among themselves. Only intervene if one puppy is bullying another too much, causing it distress and to become withdrawn.

When are puppies ready for weaning and how do I do this?

The stages of weaning are shown in the table below.

WEANING TIMETABLE

AGE	FEEDING
3–4 weeks	Puppies start to experiment with lapping at liquid foods. Strained meat broth mixed with soft cereal (such as porridge) and brown bread crumbs make suitable weaning foods. At this stage, the mixture must be smooth and runny enough for the puppies to lap up and swallow easily. Meaty and cereal baby foods are also suitable.
4–5 weeks	Progress onto more solid nourishment. Choose food specially formulated for puppies to ensure they receive the nutrients their rapidly growing bodies need. As they eat increasing amounts of solids, their excreta changes and their mother stops cleaning up after them. Now is the time to put newspaper down on the floor so that you can clean up after them easily.
5–6 weeks	Bitches naturally wean their puppies themselves as their milk gradually dries up. At this age, the puppies should be fully weaned onto solid puppy food, although they may still return to mum for the occasional comfort suckle if she allows it.

ABOVE **The mother can sometimes appear quite rough with her babies – to the point of making them squeal.**

Should puppies be vaccinated before they go to new homes?

Ideally yes, to provide them with protection against the canine diseases to which they are vulnerable. Don't forget to give the vaccination certificates to the new owners when they collect the puppies.

For details of what vaccinations puppies need, and when they should have them, see page 60.

Should I register my pedigree puppies with any organization before they go to new homes?

You only need to register pedigree puppies with the appropriate ruling kennel club if you wish to do so. You will only be able to do this if the sire and dam are also registered.

Register the puppies soon after they are born so that the registration papers arrive in time for when the pups are rehomed. You can include the cost of registration in the price of the puppies.

Why is my bitch acting as though she is pregnant, even though I know she isn't?

Also known as pseudo or phantom pregnancy, this condition is fairly common. It may occur in a bitch that has failed to conceive during a season, or has reabsorbed puppies early in a pregnancy, but thinks she is still pregnant. Pseudo pregnancies are also triggered by the bitch's hormone levels and are nature's way of ensuring that, in a pack of wild dogs or wolves, there are many bitches producing milk and capable of rearing or helping to rear a litter.

In some cases, the owner may not notice any difference in the bitch's mental or physical state, while in other bitches the false pregnancy can result in a swollen abdomen and mammary glands, which may also fill with milk. In the latter case, the bitch may also spend time nest-building and crying, and will be reluctant to exercise; she may even display the pushing actions of an actual birth. In severe cases, veterinary advice should be sought.

BELOW Some bitches experiencing a false pregnancy will form attachments to inanimate objects, such as toys, and some even have 'invisible' puppies.

I want to breed dogs professionally. Where do I start?

Read everything you can about breeding, from basic genetics onwards. Join a dog club, where you can listen to breeders discussing breeding and ask them questions. Go to dog shows and talk to breeders.

It costs as much to breed bad stock as good stock, so when you have decided which breed you like, buy the best potential breeding animals you can afford and think in terms of one or maybe two bitches. Unless you have a lot of bitches it is not a good idea to get a stud dog, as he'll need a lot of work to remain happy and healthy.

Breeding dogs can bring much personal satisfaction, but little financial reward in the long run. People who breed on a large scale purely for money do the dog world a disservice.

Do you need a licence, or permission from any canine registration organization, to breed dogs?

It depends on where you live in the world as to what regulations there are as regards breeding dogs. The best way to find out about this is to contact the regulating kennel club in your country and your local authority. The first may have restrictions on how many litters you can breed in a year, while the second may require you to obtain planning permission and a licence to operate as a breeder of dogs.

8

As dogs get older

How old is 'old' in canine terms?

There is a saying 'you are as old as you feel', and to a great extent this applies to dogs. Those that are kept fit and at their correct weight, and receive sufficient exercise, both mentally and physically, tend to stay 'younger' longer. Dogs that are overfed, underexercised and lead 'uninteresting' lives, tend to age quickly – rather like humans do.

BELOW You will notice grey areas developing on the face of dark-coated dogs as they get older.

The tables on pages 14 and 15 show which breeds do not have long lifespans, which tend to live longer than others and how old dogs are in human terms.

What are the signs of ageing?

Once your dog is beyond his prime, there will be a number of obvious signs of his decline:

- His reactions will not be as sharp.
- He won't move as quickly, nor will he be as agile.
- Depending on his character and type, he may start to rest more and be content to sit around and watch you rather than take part in whatever is going on.
- Some dogs suffer bowel and/or bladder incontinence, failing eyesight and/or hearing.
- Disturbed behaviour patterns are not uncommon, as a result of brain degeneration (the canine equivalent to Alzheimer's disease in humans).

How will I know that my dog is 'old'?

Your pet will start to slow down both mentally and physically. In many cases, this process is so gradual that you don't realize he has aged until you calculate just how many years old he is. Then you really start to notice the greying facial hair, the slow response to commands, the stiffness in his joints, the cloudy eyes and the fact that he's more likely to be a spectator than a participant in whatever is going on around him.

Will my dog require any different or special care as he ages?

An older dog is likely to tire on long walks. As he needs to keep exercising to remain as supple and fit as possible, take him for several short walks each day rather than one or two long ones. It is inevitable that his ease of movement will decline, so great care must be taken to ensure he does not become obese through lack of exercise.

Ageing dogs feel the cold: see page 230 for advice. You will probably have to revise his feed and exercise regime to help avoid 'accidents' in the house, as he won't be able to contain himself like he used to.

For advice on diet, see pages 226–227.

Are there any special foods I should be giving my old dog?

There are foods specially formulated for senior dogs. These contain all the nutrients the ageing body needs to remain in the best possible condition and to help delay or alleviate the onset of conditions such as senility.

If older dogs suffer from liver problems, a low-protein diet may be applicable; consult your vet regarding the best type of food for your dog.

Older dogs may not be as able to defend their food as they once could, so if you have other dogs make sure they are not allowed to steal his meals or intimidate him while he is eating and scare him off.

Can you insure old dogs against accident and illness?

Yes, you can, but you will need to shop around to find a pet insurance company that will cater for older dogs. Very few will take on a dog for the first time if he is 8 years old or more (depending on the breed).

Ask for sample policies from potential insurers and check the wording carefully – particularly the exclusions – to ensure the policy suits your requirements. If you do not understand anything in the policy, contact the company and ask them to explain what it means.

BELOW Giving chew treats and toys to older dogs helps to keep them gently occupied as well as promoting dental health.

Bear in mind that pre-existing ailments are not usually covered. For example, you will not be able to claim on your policy for veterinary costs incurred for arthritis treatment if your dog had the condition before you insured him.

How much exercise does an old dog need?

If your dog has remained fit and active throughout his life, carry on exercising him as normal. This is based on the idea that 'if he doesn't use it, he will lose it'.

He will tell you when he needs to slow down and, provided you are alert to your dog's needs, you will know when and how far to ease off.

Your pet's enthusiasm for walks may decrease, so reduce the length of them so as not to overtire him. However, he should still have as many (interesting) walks as possible to help prevent him becoming overweight and stiff through inactivity.

BELOW Small old dogs have the advantage over their 'big brothers' as they can be carried when they get tired on walks!

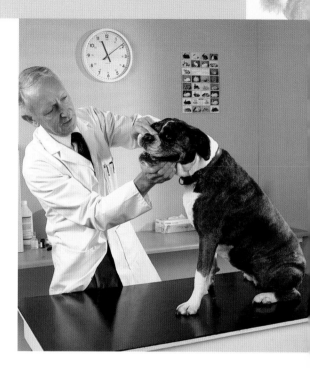

RIGHT Regular veterinary check-ups for your old dog will help nip any potential health problems in the bud.

I'd like to take on an old rescue dog – what are the advantages and/or disadvantages?

The company of an ageing dog in good health is delightful, soothing and as rewarding as playing with a puppy. His reactions may not be as sharp as a younger dog's, nor will he move as fast or be as agile when playing, but an old dog still has much to offer in that he may be well-trained, mannerly and clean in the house, and also quieter and far less demanding than a younger one.

The main disadvantage of getting an old dog is that in all likelihood you won't have as long with your pet as you would with a younger one. An old dog may also have certain undesirable habits and behaviours that are ingrained, and therefore difficult to cure. Old dogs are prone to certain 'geriatric' ailments (such as joint stiffness, dental problems and senility) that are likely to incur veterinary costs.

How can I prolong the life of my older pet?

As a dog ages, so a certain amount of body-tissue degeneration occurs. This is inevitable and cannot be prevented, although with owner and veterinary care the effects can be eased. Seek veterinary advice for any ailments your pet displays – the quicker they are dealt with, the more

likely that the outcome will be successful in prolonging you pet's life comfortably.

A suitable diet combined with appropriate exercise does wonders for maintaining health and fitness. Overtaxing your old dog with too much strenuous exercise is likely to have a detrimental effect on his health, since his ageing body is less resistant to stress and injury and will take longer to recover, using up valuable energy and resources.

Is it a good idea for my old dog to have regular veterinary examinations?

Once your dog reaches the age of 7 (or 5 if he is a giant breed), he should have a twice-yearly check-up. In this way, your vet can diagnose any problems and treat them at an early stage.

My old German Shepherd Dog has terrible hip problems. Is replacement hip surgery an option for him?

ABOVE **Many German Shepherd Dogs are prone to back and hip problems, particularly as they age.**

Unfortunately, it is unlikely that surgery will help in this case, even if you could find a vet who would agree to consider it. In addition to the increased risks involved in anaesthetizing old dogs, senior canines tend not to recover well from a major operation. In fact, it can be quite unfair to put them through surgery at all.

Putting the dog's welfare first, many vets will not consider hip replacements in elderly pets. It is judged that the pre- and post-operative trauma is unlikely to enhance the quality or length of life and could, in fact, shorten it.

Is it true that older dogs get fatter, just as humans suffer 'middle-age spread'?

Being less active as they grow older, it is easy for weight to pile on elderly canines. However, just because they are 'getting on' is no excuse to let a dog become overweight – that happens because they are fed incorrectly and/or underexercised. The same rule applies to humans!

Equally, old dogs can lose weight rapidly and starve if they are not eating for some reason, so you must keep a careful eye on an elderly pet's weight.

My old dog is putting on weight – should this be a cause for concern?

Yes, it should; being overweight puts undue strain on the heart and joints. Take your pet to the vet to find out why he is putting on weight. It could be due to something as simple as you overfeeding and/or underexercising your pet. Alternatively, an ailment could be causing the dog's weight gain: possibilities include an underactive thyroid gland (hypothyroidism), abdominal tumours, Cushing's disease (hyperadrenocortiscism), fluid retention, pregnancy in bitches, or musculosketal/heart/respiratory disease causing physical underactivity.

How can I prevent my older pet becoming obese?

Your vet will advise you on the ideal weight for your dog, and your mission is to ensure he stays at it. Weighing your dog once a week can help you monitor his weight.

To weigh your dog, weigh yourself, then pick up your dog and weigh yourself again. Subtract the first weight from the second to get your pet's weight. If your dog is large, take him to a veterinary clinic (many have weighing machines) and ask for him to be weighed.

RIGHT **Weigh out your dog's food to ensure he is receiving the correct quantity for his size and the amount of exercise he gets. Even a little too much will soon pile on the pounds.**

How can I ensure my dog remains supple and arthritis-free as he gets older?

Regular exercise helps to keep a dog comfortably mobile, as does feeding a suitable diet and managing his weight. Damage to joints is the most common cause of arthritis, either due to injury received while exercising, or because of too-rapid growth during puppyhood.

Some food supplements, known as 'chondroprotectors' (derived from fish or bovine cartilage), along with green-lipped mussel extract, which is usually available in tablet form from health food stores, are reputed to help maintain healthy joints and activate natural cartilage repair in damaged or worn joints. Some dogs have been reported to respond well to them, so ask your vet for advice about trying these with your dog.

My dog has arthritis. How I can make him more comfortable and help prevent his condition worsening?

Unfortunately, if joint degeneration occurs (either through injury or an hereditary effect or condition), causing arthritis, you cannot cure it. However, you can help to alleviate painful symptoms through the use of veterinary prescribed non-steroidal anti-inflammatory drugs (NSAIDs) to reduce joint inflammation and pain, a controlled exercise routine, an appropriate diet and managing your pet's weight. See also the advice on page 226.

It is well worth consulting a holistic vet to ascertain if any complementary medicines or therapies (such as magnetic therapy, acupuncture or herbal remedies) would help your pet. Regular swimming at a vet-recommended canine hydrotherapy centre may prove beneficial to your pet, so this is another avenue worth exploring.

Feeding your dog a cod liver oil supplement is said to help promote healthy, supple joints.

Providing your pet with a raised food bowl will make eating a more comfortable experience for him.

BELOW **You should give extra attention to cleaning and grooming a stiff old dog, as he may find self-grooming difficult if he is in pain from arthritis – pay special attention to hard-to-reach places, such as under his tail.**

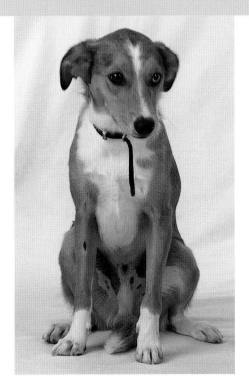

LEFT **Staring into space is a symptom of canine senility, as is disinterest in his surroundings**

What behaviour can I expect from a dog suffering from senile dementia, and how should I cope with it?

Some common symptoms are listed opposite. For example, a previously clean dog suffering from senility may have accidents in the house, making 'piles and puddles' on the floor or even on furniture (see page 239).

Just like elderly people, old dogs are resistant to and can be upset by major changes to their daily routine and lifestyle. If changes do have to happen, try to incorporate them gradually to allow your old dog time to get used to the new regime.

Seek veterinary advice if you think your pet is suffering from an age-related brain-degeneration illness. New drugs that treat chemical imbalances in the brain (which occur due to ageing) appear to be having positive effects in dogs suffering from senility, alleviating symptoms and even showing improvement in brain function, and it may be appropriate to try them on your pet.

It is worth joining a society that offers support and advice specifically for owners of senior dogs. Ask your vet and canine rescue centres/charities if they know of an appropriate organization, or have a look on the internet, keying 'senior dog society' into a search engine.

Could my dog be suffering from 'senile dementia'?

Canine senile dementia is a recognized condition in old dogs and is the equivalent of Alzeheimer's disease in humans. Symptoms include all or some of the following behaviours:

- Confusion
- Anxiety
- Abnormal sleeping patterns
- Bowel/bladder incontinence and/or abnormal toileting habits
- Disinterest in everything around him
- Forgetfulness
- Disorientation
- Irritability
- Abnormal eating behaviour (loss of appetite, or greed)
- Separation anxiety
- Abnormal vocal expression.

Should I be concerned that my old dog seems to be more 'clingy' than usual?

If your elderly dog displays an increased need for your company, make sure you give him plenty of attention and reassurance. You could even consider moving his bed into your bedroom at night if necessary.

Leaving a radio on low can help provide 'company' for your pet while you are out.

Do older dogs feel the cold more than their younger counterparts?

Elderly dogs' bodies, especially those suffering from circulatory problems, are no longer as efficient at maintaining body temperature at comfortable limits. Care must be taken, therefore, to ensure your old pet is warm enough in cold, damp weather. Both these weather elements will cause him discomfort, especially if he suffers from painful joint-related conditions such as arthritis.

My old dog has recently started waking up in the night, howling and shaking. Is he having nightmares?

This common problem in old dogs is known as 'geriatric separation anxiety'. It becomes apparent at night, when the rest of the household is asleep. The dog wakes up and feels disorientated, not knowing where everyone has gone. He starts barking and panting, showing signs of obvious anxiety; in an extreme case, he may even soil his surroundings. It is comparable to a severe panic attack in humans.

If there is no underlying physical cause for this distressing behaviour, such as a tumour, then drugs (and in some cases, alternative remedies) can be given to treat your pet's anxiety and help resolve the problem.

RIGHT **Dogs who were nervous when younger appear to be most vulnerable to geriatric separation anxiety.**

Why does my old dog not play with me like he used to?

Your dog is at a stage in his life where he feels he needs to take things more easily. This is in order to preserve his strength and energy to maintain his body's needs. You would not expect an elderly human relative to play strenuous games, nor remain busy, alert and interested from dawn until dusk, so make the same allowances for your elderly pet.

Despite his inability to play with you as he did when he was younger, your pet will gain just as much pleasure from your relationship as he always did. Although he may sit around a lot and is undemanding and quiet, an elderly dog should not be ignored. To remain happy, content and in the best possible health, he needs lots of love and affection, and exercise dependent on his physical condition, plus patience and understanding.

BELOW Make life comfortable for old dogs by equipping them with a waterproof, warm coat for outdoor exercise when the weather is cold and damp.

My old dog isn't as active as he was, so what games would be suitable and fun for us both?

Games that involve more mental than physical agility are best. You can play your dog's favourite activity games too, but on a more gentle scale so as not to tax his body too strenuously and risk injury. Reduce the length of walks (see page 224), and find new ones to maintain his interest.

Gentle tug games and training exercises that your dog can do comfortably – for example, sit, stay, fetch and shake a paw – will help keep life enjoyable for you and your pet.

I'm going on holiday – would it be fair to leave my old dog in kennels?

Provided he is fit and healthy, and is happy going into boarding kennels at holiday time, this should not present a problem. A good, caring kennels will take into account an elderly dog's needs and provide for them accordingly.

If your pet is not used to being kennelled and is not outgoing, confident and sociable by nature, or reacts badly to being separated from you, then it would be unkind to kennel him while you are away. In such cases, you will need to find an acceptable alternative (see page 233).

RIGHT If you prevail upon family, friends or neighbours to care for your pet while you are away, ensure they are sensible, reliable and competent.

BELOW Throwing treats into grass or hiding them around the house makes a great hide-and-seek game – your old dog will enjoy finding them.

What are the other options for leaving my old dog while I am away from home?

Employing a professional pet-sitter from an agency that specializes in pet care is an excellent solution. The sitter stays in your house, so you have the added advantage of home security as well as your old pet being looked after in his familiar surroundings.

If you choose this option, specify that the sitter should be experienced in caring for old dogs, to ensure your peace of mind while you are away. Never leave your old dog alone – it is not sufficient to have someone pop in once or twice a day to feed and exercise him.

My old dog has pressure sores from lying down. How can I relieve them?

Ensure your pet has plenty of soft, comfy bedding in his bed. If necessary, have several beds in different areas of the house, so that he does not have to lie on hard flooring. Beds should be easily accessible – your old pet should be able to get in and out of it without struggling to lift his bodyweight and legs.

Consult your vet as to the best way to treat your pet's pressure sores, especially if the skin is broken and sore.

My old dog sleeps more than he used to. Is this normal?

Yes, it is. Just like old people, elderly dogs need more rest in order to function as well as possible when they are active. Your dog should be allowed to rest undisturbed as and when he feels the need. Make sure that his bed is in a quiet spot in the house. Old dogs can rest and/or sleep for up to 20 hours per day.

BELOW Old dogs tend to doze their days away, preferring to be where they are most comfortable, feel safe and can therefore relax and sleep deeply.

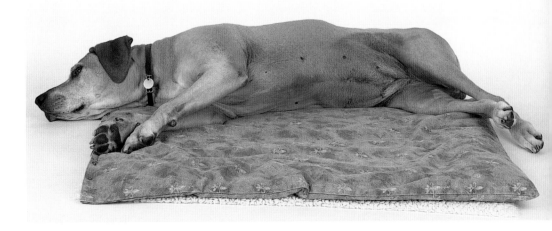

ABOVE When elderly dogs fail to respond to vocal commands and recalls, suspect that they may have problems in hearing you.

My pet is becoming grumpier and has snapped at the children. What should I do?

Your children must learn to respect your old dog's need for a quieter, calmer and less active life. He may be stiff and sore, so will not appreciate being pulled around because it will cause him discomfort and pain.

Fast-moving, loud-talking children will confuse and frighten him, so he may react uncharacteristically as a means of self-defence and in an effort to warn them to stay away from him, just as the elders in a wild dog pack would chastise unruly pups. However, although his behaviour is understandable, it is unacceptable in a domestic environment. To maintain safety all round, you need to lay down rules for your children to follow as regards their behaviour around the dog, and never leave them unsupervised with him, for all their sakes.

If, despite your efforts and the best behaviour of your children, your pet becomes unpredictable with them, you will have to consider either placing him in a suitable home without young children to stress him, or having him painlessly euthanized (see page 247).

My old dog does not respond to commands like he used to. Why?

It is likely that he has developed age-related hearing difficulties. Take him to the vet for a check-up and to ascertain if this is the case, and to see if anything can be done to correct or improve the condition.

How can I tell a deaf old dog what to do?

You will have to adapt your command signals to him so that he can understand what you want. Obviously, you cannot use your voice as he won't hear it clearly, if at all, so you will have to use other, clearly defined means by which to direct him – such as hand signals in light and flashlight signals in the dark.

Find a dog trainer who can help you devise a means of communicating with your pet visually, and then show you how to implement it effectively.

Will the fact that he cannot hear me have a detrimental effect on my old dog's life?

In general, no. However, the obvious difficulty you will have is if he goes out of your sight on walks, as he won't be able to see your visual signals to him. It is therefore important that you do not let this happen, for safety's sake – particularly if you have to recall him in a hurry.

Do not let your dog off-leash near roads, as he won't be able to hear traffic approaching, nor you calling him away from potential danger.

As regards domestic safety, make sure you do not put him in situations that might result in injury to him or other members of the family due to his deafness. For example, keep him out of the kitchen when you are cooking, and inside when you are mowing the lawn (these are wise precautions with hearing dogs, too).

BELOW With the correct training, dogs soon learn to understand and obey visual directions, such as those given by hand signals.

My old dog keeps bumping into things – could his eyesight be failing?

It most certainly could. Take him to the vet to have his eyesight checked, and to see if anything can be done to correct it – although blindness is a common and often irreversible and untreatable condition in ageing dogs.

My old dog's eyes seem to be going cloudy. Why?

This could be due to an injury, but is more likely to be eye deterioration due simply to old age. Many old dogs' eyes go cloudy, but this does not necessarily

mean that the dog is going blind, although there may be some loss of vision.

A veterinary consultation must be sought to determine the reason for your pet's eyes going cloudy, and if the condition can be treated effectively with minimum discomfort for your pet.

Can my 12-year-old Labrador Retriever's cataracts be treated successfully?

Cataracts (clouding of the lens caused through degeneration) are a common cause of impaired vision in old dogs. They are detected as a blue shadow at the back of the eye. Depending on the severity of the cataracts, dogs can still see but less clearly. If the lens appears white, then the dog will probably be blind in the affected eye(s).

Cataracts can be removed surgically and this works well for some dogs. Ask your vet for advice as to whether surgery would be appropriate in your old pet's case (see above).

My old dog is going blind. Will this affect his quality of life, and how should I cope with it?

Many dogs adapt remarkably well to being blind in one or both eyes. Provided you help him adapt to his failing eyesight,

LEFT **Cloudy or opaque eyes indicate a sight problem such as cataracts.**

your pet's quality and enjoyment of life will not be compromised.

It is important that your dog knows, via his remaining senses, that he is safe and protected, as he does not have the additional security of being able to see what he can smell, hear, taste and touch. Touching and stroking him will provide reassurance of your presence, and that you are looking out for him.

Use vocal, not visual, commands to direct him. Accustom your pet to certain walks, so that his other senses take over and he feels secure and happy on these. Elderly dogs tend to have more problems with their eyesight in bright light and in darkness, so he may be reluctant to venture out at such times.

BELOW Keep everything in the same position in the house, so that a visually impaired dog can 'mind-map' them and negotiate his way around without fear of bumping into things and injuring himself.

My old dog's nails seem longer than they used to be. Should I trim them?

Your dog may not be exercising as much as he used to on surfaces that will help to keep his nails filed down, such as pavements. Because of this, his nails will get longer. If they become so long that the dog has to compensate in movement for them, this can cause strain on other parts of the body, and on the limbs.

For nail-clipping advice, see page 63. You can also file the nails down to a more appropriate length with a tool specifically designed for the purpose (available from pet stores).

RIGHT Cutting nails after bathing is easier as the nails are softer.

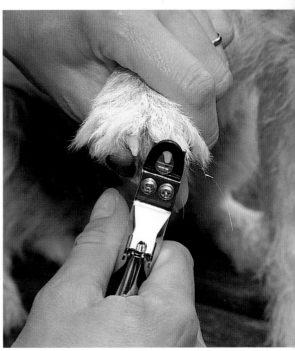

My younger dog keeps attacking the old one. How can I prevent this?

It is likely that the younger dog is bidding to become the dominant one of the two, hence his behaviour towards the old dog. Treat whichever is the dominant dog of the two as such, to maintain the pack order and help reduce friction within it. Do this by giving the 'alpha' (dominant) dog your attention (when fussing, playing, putting on the leash and so on) before the other one.

The 'underdog' will soon learn his place and accept this, while the other will then have no reason to attack him.

Separating the dogs at mealtimes is the easiest way of preventing fights breaking out over food, but give the alpha dog his meal first.

If the fighting between the two continues, consult a pet behaviourist who specializes in canines.

BELOW If you have an existing dog, consider all the pros and cons before getting a puppy.

Should I get a young dog to keep my old pet company and help keep him 'young'?

Some people consider getting a puppy when their established dog gets old. This can be a good or a bad decision, depending on the temperament and nature of the aged dog. If he likes the puppy, then he may gain a new lease of life. If he doesn't or cannot cope with the puppy's liveliness and mischievousness, then he may resent the newcomer and become depressed, withdrawn, stop eating and, ultimately, become very ill. If the old dog is the only one in the household and has always been a loner, then it would be kinder not to get another dog or puppy.

Another consideration is that as the puppy matures he is likely to exert dominance challenges over the older, weaker dog, which will make the latter's life very miserable indeed.

My 10-year-old Dalmatian is often constipated. How can I keep him comfortably 'regular'?

Constipation is an ailment of old age. It is due to decreased digestive efficiency, especially when combined with insufficient exercise. Consult your vet to ensure there is no underlying ailment causing the constipation, such as an enlarged prostate gland.

A wet or semi-moist diet containing plenty of fibre helps to keep dogs regular, as does substituting a meal once or twice a week with oily fish (tuna, pilchards, sardines). Add cod liver oil to each meal to aid the passing of motions, as well as to promote healthy joints, skin and coat.

Make sure your dog is drinking enough water – he should always have a clean, fresh supply available. Place bowls around the house and garden so that he always has easy access to it.

My ageing pet is incontinent and veterinary drug treatment seems ineffective. What can I do?

It's worth consulting a holistic vet regarding your pet's problem. Keep your dog in areas of the house where 'accidents' don't matter – but don't shut him away or limit his access to the family, as this would be unfair and cruel, as would chastizing him for something that is beyond his control. Carpets can be replaced but loving companions cannot.

You can buy 'nappies' (diapers) for dogs which are worth trying, and also special 'stay dry' bed pads that soak up urine leakage.

Clean up urine with products that are designed to remove stains and odour – these are available from pet stores.

My 12-year-old Yorkshire Terrier has recently started having trouble eating. What could be the matter with him?

The first thing to check is your pet's mouth for signs of an ailment, such as a tumour, gingivitis or an abscess. Take him to the vet for an all-over check-up. If he gets a clean bill of health, change his food to one designed for old dogs and which is easier for him to chew. Moist food served at room temperature is more appetizing, as well as easier and more comfortable for ageing teeth to deal with.

Feed two or three small meals a day rather than one or two larger ones. A few tempting morsels in the food or gravy to soften it and add interest should prove hard to resist.

My old dog is drinking more water than usual. Is this abnormal?

Excessive thirst (polydipsia) is always a cause for concern, so take your pet to the vet for a check-up. Reasons for drinking more water than normal include diabetes mellitus (sugar diabetes) and renal failure, both of which are ailments that commonly affect old dogs.

How can I keep my older dog comfortable when travelling in the car?

For basic advice on transporting dogs, see page 56. In addition, there are several other precautions you can take:
● Take frequent breaks, in a safe place, so that your old dog can stretch his legs to alleviate stiffness and to toilet.
● Avoid long journeys wherever possible.
● Smooth driving is a must, especially around corners, particularly as old dogs tend not to be as well able to balance as younger ones.

ABOVE A dental problem may be the cause of a dog going off his food.

● Provide comfy, thick bedding for your dog to lie on.
● Help keep him occupied with a hollow Kong toy stuffed with soft cheese and treats, or potted meat spread.

My old dog has difficulty jumping in and out of the car, and he's too heavy to lift. How can I solve this problem?

The easiest solution is to put a gently sloping ramp up to the back/side door of the car for your dog to walk up. The ramp should be sturdy and covered with non-slip material for sure footing. Wood planks or even an old door might do.

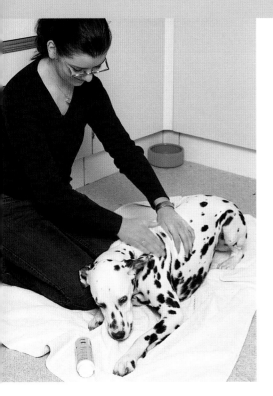

ABOVE **Using a dry shampoo is easier than bathing your dog in water.**

How can I cure my old dog's awful body odour?

There are a number of possible causes of, and therefore solutions to, this problem. These are shown in the table below.

My old dog is terrified of loud noises, especially fireworks. How can I alleviate his fear?

Most animals are terrified of fireworks and other loud noises. There are a number of steps you can take:

● If fireworks are going off in the neighbourhood, keep your dog safely indoors. Turn on the TV or radio to help drown out the noise of fireworks (or thunder).

● Cover your dog's bed or crate to make a 'den' to which he can escape and feel safe.

BODY ODOUR

CAUSE	SOLUTION
Flatulence	Try changing your pet's diet to a more natural one.
Some veterinary drugs	Consult your vet.
Skin ailments	Consult your vet.
Overproductive oil glands	Bath your dog regularly.
Poor oral hygiene	Regular dental check-ups and cleaning are recommended. Give your dog hide chews, toys and large, raw, meaty bones to help clean his teeth and gums.
Blocked anal sacs	Consult your vet.

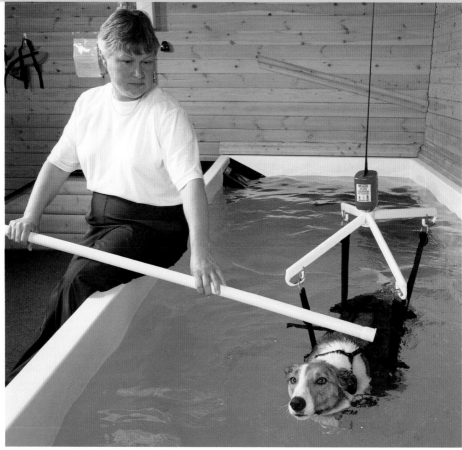

ABOVE Swimming at a reputable canine hydrotherapy pool, as recommended by a vet, can help alleviate stiffness and promote mobility for older dogs.

● Do not reassure or comfort her when loud noises occur, as this will only serve to reinforce her fears. Simply ignore her, and carry on with what you are doing. If you do not display anxiety, she is less likely to become anxious herself. Only give her attention if she shows confident behaviour.

● Using a rescue remedy (based on flower essences and available from health food shops) can help keep dogs calm, as can giving your pet a soothing massage.

● Noise desensitization tapes or CDs can sometimes help and these are available from good pet stores, or ask your vet for details of where you might obtain them.

Would swimming help to ease my old pet's stiffness?

Hydrotherapy can be of benefit to all dogs suffering from mobility problems. This is because it enables dogs to exercise without exerting undue stress on their joints. Ask your vet for a referral to a reputable centre for dogs that is within a reasonable distance for regular visits.

A good centre will:

● Only take dogs on veterinary referral.

● Have suitable accident and third party liability insurance.

● Have experienced staff trained in canine first aid.

● Provide a heated pool large enough to cater for all sizes of dog, which has swim jets to increase the water flow as necessary, a safety pet harness, and a means of getting the dog into the water easily.

Is it true that 'you cannot teach an old dog new tricks'?

No, elderly pets enjoy learning new things just as much as young ones. They get a good deal of pleasure from mastering a task or puzzle and then being rewarded for it.

As with younger dogs, be careful not to reward undesirable behaviour, since the old dog will then view what he did as acceptable and do it again. Ignore behaviours you don't want him to make a habit of and reward those you do wish to be repeated.

My 9-year-old dog recently developed a heart murmur. What can be done?

This is a serious condition and requires appropriate veterinary treatment, depending on the cause. Heart problems usually arise because of irregular rhythm or valve disease. Consult your vet for advice on treatment.

The good news is that treatment is usually successful in maintaining a good, relatively discomfort-free quality of life for your pet, and is made up of a combination of providing a suitable diet, maintaining a healthy weight, reducing exercise and medication.

BELOW Maintaining mental and physical activity helps to keep old dogs 'younger' for longer.

Is it true that shiatsu is especially beneficial for elderly dogs?

Shiatsu (finger pressure therapy) stimulates muscle relaxation and blood circulation. It encourages the body to self-heal, so is indeed beneficial for elderly canines.

BELOW Some dogs enjoy shiatsu, others do not – your pet will tell you if it's an appropriate treatment for him.

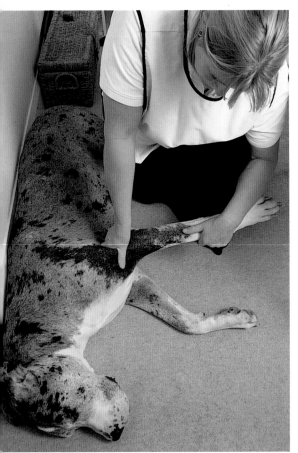

Ask your vet to recommend a shiatsu practitioner. Alternatively, you can try it yourself – invest in a good 'how-to' book on practising the technique on your pet.

How can I prevent my old dog, whose mobility is restricted, from falling on the stairs when I'm not there?

For his own safety, your dog must not be allowed to negotiate stairs unaided. You must therefore make them inaccessible to him when you are not there to supervise.

Some dogs are miserable when prevented from going upstairs 'to bed' with their owners, if they have been used to doing so. In this case, consider moving your bed downstairs to be with him – especially if your old pet is not likely to be with you for much longer.

BELOW A stair gate will prevent an elderly dog from falling down the stairs.

My old dog has recently become snappy, particularly if I try to pick him up. Why?

Your dog is probably suffering from pain or discomfort, which is exacerbated when you pick him up. A thorough examination by a vet will determine the cause, so that a solution can, hopefully, be found to ease your pet's distress.

BELOW **Using a towel or body warmer is a cheap and effective way of lending your dog mobility support.**

Why has my pet started snoring when asleep?

Flat-faced (brachycephalic) breeds are prone to snoring due to their deformed mouth structure. If this is not the case with your pet, there are some other possible reasons:

- Obesity
- Loose tissue in the throat
- An obstruction in the throat
- A reaction to a substance in the atmosphere, such as cigarette smoke.

A veterinary inspection will help to determine the cause, and ensure that appropriate treatment is given as necessary. It may also help to change your pet's bed for a larger or different-shaped one, so that he can sleep in a different position.

My dog suffers from a degenerative spinal disease. How can I help him to get around?

Make a non-slip and comfortable sling to place under your dog's tummy using a towel. As he pulls himself along with his forelegs, you can support his hindquarters easily and without straining your back. Lower the sling slightly to allow him to relieve himself when required.

On tiled and wooden floors, put down a non-slip floor covering such as carpet, to help prevent your dog slipping on them – such flooring surfaces are a major cause of limb and back injury suffered by elderly dogs.

My old pet pants a lot. Why?

An older dog's circulatory system is not as efficient at maintaining body temperature as it once was (see page 230). When he is too warm, he'll pant to expel heat from his body via evaporation of moisture from his tongue, thereby lowering his body temperature.

If your dog is suffering from a heart or lung problem, panting is a result of him trying to draw enough oxygen into his body to survive. If he's stressed, he'll use up more oxygen, so will pant to provide himself with more.

If your pet appears distressed when panting, seek veterinary advice.

ABOVE A dog pants to help cool himself down, inhale enough oxygen or when he's stressed.

I know my pet's days are numbered. How can I make our remaining time together as happy as possible?

Dogs are quick to pick up on their owners' emotions. At this time in your and your dog's life, you must be easy on yourself and think positively, and make the most of your time together with your pet. If you are buoyant, your pet will be too; if you are unhappy, so will he be – and that's the last thing you would want for him.

Don't dwell on the fact that your old dog won't be with you for much longer. Instead, make the most of each day with him. For example, play the games he enjoys most, take him to the beach on a fine, warm day, give him his favourite treats, and generally spoil him rotten – at this stage in his life, it doesn't matter if he gets a bit tubbier. Making your dog's last days special will make you feel better, and he will certainly appreciate it.

Take lots of photos (and video films if possible) of him enjoying himself, so that you will have good, visual memories of him.

How will I know when the time is right to have my old dog 'put to sleep'?

Eventually, the older dog sleeps more and more and is increasingly reluctant to exercise. While he is able to function normally, if only in this modified way, he is probably quite happy and contented.

If your pet's bladder, bowels and limbs begin to fail, and he is unable to function without mental distress or physical pain, the only humane thing to do is to have your old friend euthanized, allowing him to die painlessly and with dignity. It's the last kind thing you can do for a much-loved companion.

RIGHT Although it's not pleasant to think about, it is wise at this time to consult your vet and discuss when and where your pet's euthanasia will take place. Being prepared makes it easier for both of you when the time comes.

What happens when a dog is euthanized and should this be done at home or at the vet's?

Properly carried out, the process is quick and relatively painless:

1 A sedative injection may be given if necessary.

2 A foreleg is usually shaved to identify where the relevant vein is situated.

3 An injection is given in this vein, comprising an overdose of anaesthetic. This causes the dog to become drowsy, lapse into unconsciousness and die peacefully in seconds.

If the dog's circulatory system isn't working efficiently, the vet may need to inject directly into the heart or kidneys. Owners can find this method distressing, and this is where an experienced and sympathetic vet nurse proves an invaluable help to all concerned.

BELOW A grave to mark where your pet lies can prove therapeutic. You will have somewhere tangible to go to mourn your pet, and then remember him with gladness when your grief subsides.

If you can arrange for both a vet and a vet nurse to come to your home, then this is ideal. Otherwise, it is best to take your pet to the clinic at a pre-booked quiet time (usually the last appointment of the surgery). Have someone go with you for support and to drive.

What happens to the dog after he has been euthanized?

The vet will dispose of the body or arrange to have it buried or cremated on your instructions. Alternatively, you can take your pet home to bury him in a favoured area of the garden, if this is allowed in your area. Graves should be at least 1 m (3 ft) deep and well away from water courses – your local environment agency will advise. If you decide to have your pet cremated, pet cemeteries and crematoria will advise you on cost and what is involved.

My pet died some weeks ago, but I am still finding it hard to cope. Is this normal?

Grieving is an essential part of the healing process after bereavement. There is no set time limit as to how long owners grieve for their pet: some are able to accept and recover from the loss more easily than others, who may not get over it for months, even years – this is perfectly normal. However long it takes, do not be afraid to grieve when you feel the need. Bottling up grief will affect your own mental and physical health.

I feel guilty that I had my old dog euthanized. Should I have done more to save him?

Sometimes owners cannot bear to lose their pet. This is understandable, but means they put off having the dog put down when really it should be done sooner rather than later. However, a caring owner will put their pet's needs first, not their own – no matter the cost to themselves.

Many owners blame themselves for their pet's death, and agonize over whether it could have been prevented if they had 'done things differently or tried harder to save him', when in fact there was nothing further that could be done. This is a normal reaction, but sadly it cannot change what has happened.

It is important, for your own sake, to focus on the many happy times you enjoyed with your cherished pet, and to hold and treasure those memories.

Will getting another dog help me to cope with the death of my old one?

After the death of a dog, do not get another one just to help you cope with the death of your old pet. If you want to get another dog, wait until you feel emotionally and physically ready to cope with a new addition to the household.

If you have other pets, perhaps the last thing you need right now are the potential problems that introducing a new dog into the equation may bring. Wait until a little time has passed.

BELOW Sometimes it helps to get another dog soon after losing one, but doing so without careful consideration can be a mistake.

ABOVE Never underestimate a child's grief or reaction to the death of a pet, as it can affect them in many different ways. These may have long-lasting and detrimental effects on their behaviour, health, learning ability and socialization. As a parent or guardian, it is important to provide them with support and understanding.

Could my other dog and even the cat be grieving over the loss of their canine friend?

It is not just the owner who grieves over the loss of a pet – other animals in the household can too. Some people prefer to let the other animals see the body of their friend, so that they recognize he has died and 'say goodbye'.

The best thing to do is to carry on with the remaining pets' routine as normal, and to let them work out a new hierarchy among themselves.

How can I make our dog's death easier for my two children?

Depending on their age, children react differently to the death of a pet. For many, it will the first time they experience this. It will help enormously if you talk things through with a bereavement counsellor as regards how to approach and explain pet death to your children. They, too, may find such supportive third-party help invaluable.

One thing you should not do is say that the pet was 'put to sleep', as this can create false hope – the child may think that one day their doggy friend will wake up and come back again.

As to whether a child should be allowed to see the body of the pet, this again depends on the age and psyche of the particular child, and a qualified counsellor will be able to advise on the best course of action.

BELOW **By making provision for their pet should they predecease him, many elderly people can enjoy the pleasure and comfort a dog provides until they die.**

I am elderly and would love a dog for company. How can I ensure he will be well looked after if I die before he does?

A relative may be willing to give the dog a good home. If not, some animal charities will take on this responsibility and find the dog a home of which you would have approved. To ensure this happens in event of your death, contact a charity that makes such provisions to find out what you need to do beforehand. When the time comes the dog can be transferred to the charity or new home with the minimum of fuss and stress.

Index

Acknowledgements

Main photography by © Octopus Publishing Group Limited/Angus Murray.

Alamy/David Crausby 116 bottom left.
Animal Photography/Sally Anne Thompson 173 bottom right.
Ardea/John Daniels 161 top, 200 top; /M. Watson 99 bottom.
Corbis UK Limited/Ed Bock 224 bottom; /Philip James Corwin 125 right; /Ronnie Kaufman 143 right; /Tom Nebbia 126; /Ariel Skelley 146 top left.
John Daniels 106 bottom right, 191 bottom left, 210 bottom, 225 top right, 242 top, 244 bottom right.
DK Images 15 picture 8.
Empics/Tim Ockenden 189 bottom.
Frank Lane Picture Agency 208 bottom; /David T. Grewcock 195 bottom right, 248 bottom left; /David Hosking 180 bottom left, 236 bottom left, 237 centre right; /Gerard Lacz 207 top; /Roger Tidman 86 bottom left, 145 bottom right; /Martin Withers 196 bottom right.
Getty Images/Greg Ceo 251 bottom; /Tim Davis Cover wraparound; /Sean Murphy 29.
Octopus Publishing Group Limited 191 top; /Frank Adam 92 bottom right; /Colin Bowling 170 top left; /Jane Burton 166 bottom; /Stephen Conroy 87 centre right, 203 centre right; /John Daniels 52; /Steve Gorton 6 top right, 6 bottom right, 6 bottom centre left, 6 top centre right, 13, 17, 20 picture 3, 27, 28, 43, 49, 50, 56, 57, 60, 74, 76, 83, 85 top left, 100 top left, 102, 104 bottom left, 105, 120 right, 123, 124 top, 133, 158, 164 bottom right, 176 bottom right, 185 bottom left, 194 bottom left, 213 bottom, 216, 220, 221 top, 232 bottom left, 243 bottom right, 246, 249 right, 250 top; /Rosie Hyde 1, 6 top left, 6 bottom centre right, 6 top centre left, 8, 9 top, 44, 45 top, 45 bottom left, 46 right, 51, 54 left, 55, 62, 63, 64, 69, 94 top left, 94 top right, 101 bottom, 103 bottom right, 109 right, 113, 115, 117, 125 left, 127 bottom, 129 top, 131 bottom left, 137 bottom, 138 bottom right, 150 bottom, 190, 191 bottom right, 193 top, 201 bottom right, 202 bottom, 212 top, 215 top, 223 bottom right, 238 bottom; /Jane Burton 70–71; /William Lingwood 180 bottom right; /Peter Loughran 199 bottom; /Ray Moller 2 top centre, 2 top left, 2 top right, 2 bottom right, 2 bottom left, 2 bottom centre, 2 centre right top, 2 centre right bottom, 2 centre left bottom, 2 top centre left, 2 centre top, 9 bottom right, 9 bottom left, 10–43, 12 left, 12 right, 15 picture 9, 15 picture 7, 15 picture 6, 15 picture 5, 15 picture 4, 15 picture 3, 15 picture 2, 15 picture 1, 16, 18, 20 picture 6, 20 picture 5, 20 picture 4, 20 picture 1, 21 left, 21 right, 22, 24, 26, 30 picture 5, 30 picture 4, 30 picture 3, 30 picture 2, 30 picture 1, 31, 32 picture 3, 32 picture 2, 32 picture 1, 33, 35 left, 35 right, 35 centre, 39 left, 39 right, 41, 46–75, 78–101, 104–129, 160–189, 192, 195 bottom left, 222; /Tim Ridley 34, 47, 81 top left, 122, 132, 134 top right, 184 top right, 187 bottom, 222 bottom left, 229 top left, 230 bottom right, 232 bottom right, 233 bottom; /L Wickenden 87 top centre, 87 top left, 87 top right.
Angela Hampton/Family Life Picture Library 36, 37 picture 1, 54 right, 91 bottom right, 97 centre right, 103 top, 112 right, 121, 131 bottom right, 156 bottom left, 163 bottom right, 165 bottom left, 172 top right, 176 bottom left, 206 bottom, 209 top, 211 top right, 217 top, 221 bottom right, 221 bottom left, 231 bottom, 244 bottom left, 247 bottom right.
Marc Henrie/Kennel Club 61.
James McKay 116 bottom right, 181 bottom left.
The Kennel Club/Carol Ann Johnson 77 top.
N.H.P.A./Henry Ausloos 159 bottom left, 178 bottom left; /Ernie Janes 237 bottom right.
Photolibrary.com 91 top right, 107 bottom right; /Oxford Scientific/J. L. Klein/M. L. Hubert 228 bottom.
Warren Photographic 97 top, /Jane Burton 37 picture 3, 37 picture 2, 177 bottom, 204 bottom left, 205 bottom, 245 bottom left.
Your Dog Magazine 53, 159 bottom right, 173 bottom left, 201 top right, 203 bottom right, 241 top left.

Executive Editor Trevor Davies
Project Editor Charlotte Wilson
Executive Art Editor Karen Sawyer
Designer Peter Gerrish
Production Manager Ian Paton
Picture Researcher Sophie Delpech